I Am The Quiet

Of The Falling Snow

A Spiritual and
Transformational Journey Through Loss

Aspen Bernath-Plaisted

Cover art and photo by Tim Bernath-Plaisted

First Printing 2012

ISBN 978-0-9852284-0-8

Published by Turtle Creek Artisans   2012

www.TurtleCreekArtisans.com

In Memory Of My Parents

Leonard and Sylvia who offered me all of the love that a daughter could need along with enough challenge from which to forge my spiritual transformational journey. And so I journey on...
I love and miss you both dearly.

I would like to dedicate this book

To My husband Tim, who has been more to me than anyone could ever hope for. Who has worked relentlessly lending all his gifts toward this project of creating a book, and patiently producing for me exactly what I had requested, even if it meant another re-do. I don't know where you came from, but thank-you for coming to me. I love you dearly and forever.

To Shandra and Jacy, with whom I have the privilege and joy to call my daughter and son. Thank you for being who you are and supporting me in who I am. I waited a long time for you, but it was worth the wait! I love you completely and exactly as you are.

To my sister Renee, who continuously proves the depth of sisterly love, protectiveness, and support. It is true that there is nothing like a sister. I am filled with much love and gratitude for you.

My love is unending.

Table of Contents

Poems

i

$\mathcal{A}$ Note to the Reader

Dear Reader,

I feel I owe you a bit of an explanation about the format of my book. First, I would like to explain that although I do not label this book as being *channeled* in the traditional use of the word, it did come to me in the way that all of my writings have been available to me throughout my life. My poems usually present themselves as a title, which suggests that it is time to sit and do my *inner listening* which allows the rest to follow. I do this type of listening whenever I have the need or am moved to *know* something.

This book was not my idea. I did not think to myself that I should begin a book. It surfaced in my mind and I accepted the calling. You will notice that most of the included poems were written years before the onset of this book. I believe they were simply in a state of stasis, waiting for when they were needed. I was thrilled to see how they became the current that guided the flow of this writing. Though this book has the umbrella effect of being linear and chronological in the sense that it begins at an earlier date and travels to a later date, I hope you will permit the leaps of time that it takes in between. Perhaps you could take a leap of faith with it and see where it leads.

Next is the question of genre. Like myself, there is probably no one box in which to label its style. It resembles a memoir in that I share stories, the section about my father being very personal and truly telling my story. However, as with my private work with clients, my stories are meant as a vehicle for delivering philosophical and spiritual thoughts, with the hope of shifting perspective and changing awareness. It is my greatest desire that these thoughts will inspire you, perhaps awaken your truths, and serve to lovingly motivate you to lift your quality of existence to whatever the next step is for you. To know that would, in itself, bring me great joy.

Finally, since this book has been a gift to me, I am inclined to just allow it to be what it is. It is my greatest hope that you, the reader, will do the same.

With much love and peace,
Aspen

*I*ntroduction

I am in my study, newly built, a new addition to our home and what has become a ceremonial shrine for me. As I walk through the hallway and open the door I enter an oasis of peace and spiritual communion. " I am, and that is it." In this shrine of awakening to self that is good enough. It may sound simple or trite, but that is how it works for me. The addition was built and I prepared and performed a ceremony. I danced with my animal spirits and kin, called upon my ancestors and teachers, and asked for all helping entities and the energies of light and love to come, and help bless me and this new space. So they did. It was wonderful. Now, when I enter this room I feel their blessing and so I am at peace.

One year, for my birthday, Tim and the children bought me a new green leather-bound journal. I loved it! I was so attracted to the beauty of the rich green cover with the softly floating whales etched into it. I love journals, but I was afraid to touch it. I looked at it with growing longing each day. It taunted me and called to me. I wanted to open it up and write, but I knew it had to be something special. What should it be? Not another self-help book. What could I possibly say that has not already been said? Yet a stirring continued to grow inside. I have a story to write. My story. I do not know whether it is new or different or interesting enough to share, but it is my story to be written honestly and from the heart.

I sat on the floor and once again called in my teachers and guides. I explained that I felt I was supposed to begin. The previous night I experienced a very restless night's sleep. When I awoke I felt a familiar energy of anticipation and knew that it was time to begin. Maybe it was to be for my healing, and maybe also to help others in their healing; I was not certain. I asked for a sign that would help me to understand my "assignment" and suddenly I was sobbing. Yes, my story is valuable. That is the end, no critical judgments. I, myself, devoid of all old standards or images, preconceived ideas, and old ideas about perfections. I was to shed and release all of the old layers. I am, and that is enough. That was the message. So now I open this green leather-bound journal without hesitation, because I have something to say that comes from the deepest and ageless part of me.

Looking out beyond the curtain-less windows, I felt that I had the whole expanse with which to watch the falling snow. Now, remembering the words given to me at my medicine wheel when seeking guidance, *I truly am the quiet of the fallingsnow*. With this quiet and with love I begin...

I Am The Quiet

Of The falling Snow

Angel Wings

Love can be like that.
Yes, I remember making angel wings in the snow.
As a child, everything seeming so much bigger than life.
And I never got cold,
warmed by the energy of play and love.

Yes, love can be like that.
I remember my mom calling me into the house and I
walked in all dripping of snow and ice.
Rosy cheeks and frozen toes.
She'd help to undress me, and I'd sit by the heater
warming my feet and drinking hot milk.
Rub my toes, please.

Yes, love can be like that.
Well, making angel wings is probably even more fun
than building a snowman. A snowman just melts, but
ANGEL WINGS TAKE FLIGHT.
LIMITLESS, THEY KNOW NO BOUNDARIES,
just vapors breaking free.

Yes, love can be like that.
Funny thing, they leave their landing mark.
A mere outline of what was once there.
A melted shadow announcing a joyous commitment to return.
Twinkling fairy lights showing off the sky,
 and blessing my life.

YES, LOVE CAN BE LIKE THAT.

1985

I Am The Quiet Of The Falling Snow

*C*HILDHOOD- SOME TIME, *some year*

Like all children I experienced the quiet magic of the falling snow frequently throughout the years of many Michigan winters. Waking up and feeling the stillness around me, then jumping up gleefully, quite certain that I would find a white and soft world waiting for me just beyond the window shade. I stood up on my bed, up on my toes, and peered out. My faith was rewarded with immediate joy, and often with the news that school was canceled for the day.

Life was miraculous, I knew even then. At least my body did. I had a strong body *knowing* that would fill me with a combination of awe, happiness, and wonder. I would often think that my body knew something that my mind simply could not comprehend. Somehow I knew that was okay. Later in life I learned to read books on difficult subjects and would simply let my body comprehend. That was enough. The information always seemed to get where it needed to be, and in turn I was where I needed to be. In many ways trust was easy for me as a child. Life was very secure and straightforward, and love was strongly present. Right and wrong, justice, human rights compassion and respect, were very black and white for me and not subjects to be debated. I trusted in myself and in my judgments, even if I did find myself a loner from time to time because of this. That doesn't mean that I avoided the complete set of insecurities that most of us go through as adolescents. Hardly! Yet, on another level, when it came down to living life I rarely doubted or hesitated about what to do. Inner values and standards were already the guiding force. Though I don't recall taking the time to actually define this force, it was seldom denied. There are no right or wrong courses in life since all paths will serve as opportunities for growing. However, following one's internal designs or truths can hasten our awakening to our true selves and consequently lead to a more quality experience of life on earth.

I went through times of feeling friendless and sad about the harshness which children so easily showed to one another. I was lucky not to be one who was ridiculed, but I hated to witness the level of demeaning behavior that was often hurled towards other kids. Evenings marked many tearful conversations with my father about this dilemma. He became my cornerstone of unconditional love and encouragement. He advised me to remain true to myself and my ideal for love in the world, and so I have throughout my life thus far.

I often look back on my early years in elementary school and review my somewhat difficult adjustment with my peers, as well as my fears and discontentment and dislike for authority. I was just unable to buy into or adopt someone else's truths as was expected for a child to do. Children were simply "supposed" to become extensions of their families, culture, and society at large. This is comfortably referred to as "socialization." For those who failed to accept that plan they often experienced bumps in the road. In the course of my growing up, my mom received most of the backlash and bumps from me about that.

Of course, she was the main authority in my life who tried to mold and shape me to fit her life's view. I felt badly about those "bumps" with my mom, and from time to time I attempted to even things out. I even prayed about it, though at the time I had not the slightest belief in whom or what I was praying to since organized religion did not work for me and I was not encouraged to discover my own spirituality. Hence, my most common prayer went as follows: " Dear God, if you are there, please forgive me for not believing in you. Please help me to be the good traditional Jewish girl that my mother wants me to be. And please help me to be nicer to my her." I really meant it, but I never felt heard.

What I wasn't aware of at the time was the idea that we all brought with us to each lifetime a whole package complete with desires, directions, standards, ethics, ideals, potentials, and dormant knowledge and memories. Those underlying messages would manifest themselves in the form of what could be called natural tendencies and longings. The truth is that in my early youth I just was not ready to be here on Earth and have to give up so much. At some level I wasn't sure that life on earth could meet the very high standards that my soul remembered and I craved.

It wasn't hard to follow my own way or path. In fact, it didn't seem to be a question. It was just that way and I just was. I did not look for a philosophy or a label to wear. I had plenty of regular things in life to be self-conscious about. My clothes were not new and I was too skinny to look good in any of them, and my hair was curly and hard to manage. My dad tried to cheer me up on numerous occasions by insisting that I was not skinny, "just lean!" Many other fears kept me awake at night as I remained in bed with the covers tightly wrapped around my head with just barely enough oxygen allowed in for breath. Still, my direction was clear. My simple life was intact; I existed, Dad continued to love me, and so did Mom, miraculously even if I did cause her grief, and so my feet walked on this earth with some trepidation about being here but always fairly certain as to where they were going. They were going home to *self*. The journey towards discovering the true self is not openly outlined, nor are all the details known. The details, mediums, tools and resources all change throughout the course of a lifetime, but the destination remains true.

Circle Dance

I knew an old woman who lived by the sea.
She often spoke of the whales to me.
She said, "Don't you see, don't you see,
the life of each whale is sacred and precious to me."

I once knew an old man, he lived in the hills.
He often spoke of the mountain goat.
He said, "Don't you see, don't you see,
the life of each mountain goat is sacred and precious to me."

I once knew a child, she lived in the woods.
She often spoke of the deer to me.
She said, "Don't you see, don't you see,
the life of each deer is sacred and precious to me."

I said, "Take this hand and this one too,
and join in the circle dance that we do.
Yes, take this hand and this one too,
 and join in the circle dance that we do."

I knew many mothers who lived overseas,
they often spoke of the hunger to me.
They said, "Don't you see, don't you see,
the life of each child is sacred and precious to we."

I said, "Take this hand and this one too,
and join in the circle dance that we do.
Yes, take this hand and this one too
and join in the circle dance that we do."

1984

$\mathcal{T}$HE EVOLVING CIRCLE

There was a time when the world was thought to be flat. However, the news that it is round is no longer news. So it is with life here on earth so long considered to be linear. It seems fairly old hat these days to say that life is a circle of relationships and dimensions, each interpreted as separate realities. In fact, these thoughts could be referred to as "old age" since many of the ancient and indigenous civilizations shared in that thinking. So as today's "new age" blends with the old age thinking, there is one full circle to consider. I write this very simply here, as the scientific details cannot be my job. I am not a physicist. Remember, my body's cellular intelligence and memories understand much more than my words can tell you. I was once embarrassed and concerned about that. I am no longer. There, from self-doubt I also go full circle to when I was a child and trusted what I carried within even without a sophisticated understanding of the details. I like circles. To live a circle is to live a life of no regrets. There are always opportunities for learning and re-learning and using what you've learned. The present will intersect with the past as we walk the circle. If enough self-forgiveness and healing has occurred, which promotes forgiveness and compassion for one's self and of others, as we then rendezvous with points from the past healing is facilitated. In that way we can make a jump up the spiral of personal healing and spiritual awareness.

Moving to another point on my circle I gaze out the window again. The snow is still falling and I can't resist going out for a while. The kids are already sledding. While piling on my clothing, I think about personal changes occurring for me, such as the continual letting-go process of thoughts that are not beneficial. For example, releasing old ideas of how I should look, and shedding old concepts of physical limitations due to old injuries and such, I can focus more on the freedom of playing and being alive and physical in my body.

That is an enjoyable change. I like it and I love sledding! My mind continues to drift back to memories of other times. Times when restraints and images have won out. It feels good to have moved on. It feels strange to compose these memories while in the present moment. Sometimes it is difficult to discern whether I am at the beginning of the journey or the end. A brief slip into purely linear viewing, and then I remember: I am the journey; in each evolving moment, I am. There is no beginning and there is no end. There is only the journey.

As I continue on this evolving and revolving circle of life a great tunnel opens up and forms a bridge to myself at other points of time. It feels good to travel across that bridge and access a new understanding and awakening to my personal story. The awakening takes me to a higher level of functioning in my present daily existence. So, taking a deep breath and feeling my quiet, I travel across to another realm. Heart and mind join together in waves of high-spirited emotions, dramatizing memories and drawing new, fuller dimensional pictures based on a higher understanding that is no longer flat. Hindsight does have its value!

As an adolescent and teenager I felt the *calling* of my spiritual self. It wasn't a direct call; angels didn't appear and take me under their wing, but it was a calling. I heard it somewhere. Maybe that's what rebellion is truly about. Sometimes misguided, but perhaps it is a desperate attempt to be true to self, which sometimes can seem to require the rejection of traditional or socialized flat thinking. Now, as a parent, that gives me something to ponder about for my own children. What have we lost in this Western culture which

calls upon the work ethic so strongly that our worth is measured by our product and deviation from the norm is either frowned upon or assimilated? For most, the desire to rebel, or return to self, is later overruled by a stronger need for approval and acceptance. The price paid for that assimilation becomes insidiously buried within over time.

My teenage years were surprisingly glorious. They were fun filled with successful friendships, and I was both trusted by my parents and respected by my teachers. In the midst of a mainstream existence and normal peer pressures, I somehow managed to walk a fairly true line. Truth, honesty, and integrity remained highly important to me. Intuitively I carved a comfortable path, including holding true to myself, already filled with aspirations and high ideals, while at the same time I enjoyed the privilege of youth. I often think of children less fortunate than myself, born into poverty and/or war or other circumstances of despair and hopelessness. Those children are forced to grow up quickly and are denied or deprived of the opportunity to flourish with an air of lightness while still in their youth. More and more that seems to be the case of our society's youth as we watch them floundering, not with lightness of heart but with a carelessness that often comes from broken threads of spiritual relationships, resulting in a loss of personal connection to self. For those youth and soon-to-be adults, a journey to self can mean the retrieving of heart and spirit.

I can see now that this thread of spiritual guidance that has been with me forever was indeed from the fiber which forms an invisible link throughout the entire circle of life. It was and is the energetic network that connects all beings and makes higher guidance available to all of us. I am so thankful for that. It was common for me to feel a joi de vie (joy of life) while at the same time having the feeling that there was something more. I responded to this feeling that something was missing with the need and desire to live an exciting and non-ordinary life. Later in life that desire sometimes presented itself as a feeling of being restless or discontented. It seemed there was something more that I was to be doing with my life. Later still, I began to recognize this restless stirring as information coming to me from that vast information highway (non-verbal/intuitive or higher understanding) that so often ends up in a traffic jam. I have found that it is the most significant and most vital information that will repeatedly attempt a breakthrough. So I learned to be quiet and listen. In this quiet the threads of connection remain whole, the bridge to oneness remains accessible, and life becomes meaningful. With my quest for meaning I was attracted to those who didn't seem to fit in, either because of special needs or requirements for life, or simply because they walked their own path. I didn't realize at the time that I, too, had been walking my own path. I was not choosing to defy, I was simply listening and in this listening one simply becomes.

I Am The Quiet Of The Falling Snow

Voices of Myself

Listen, shh, listen.
Who's there?
It is I.
Who?

Listen, shh, listen.
Who's there?
It is you.
Who?

We are one.
What do you want?
Peace, love, unity.
How?

Shh, listen.

1981

$\mathcal{B}$ ECOMING POWERFUL

I have listened a lot throughout my life. I listened to the stirring in my heart, to the understanding pulsing through my body, and to the awe and wonder that grew inside of me about life. I listened to my direction calling me to nature, calling me to the animals, to the trees, and to the Earth, our mother. I'd gaze at the top of trees, brilliant in their green beauty contrasting against hues reflected by a blue sky, and then would grow dizzy as the arms of the tree ballerina swayed slowly in the breeze. At other times they were stark winter branches, sharp with a graceful strength.

I listened with a saddened heart when race riots broke out in my high school. In my naiveté I marveled at how it all started, this inhumanity to life on earth. Then I was angered because my life was being jarred. My small life was being forced to stretch beyond its comfortable horizon. I struggled with my pain as my world expanded to understand in a real and tangible way that there were so many who lived without. Without justice, without love, without the peace of mind of knowing that they and their loved ones were safe. I still think of that as an adult. Driving down the road I may see a child of an ethnic minority, walking about. Suddenly, I am acutely taken by pain from the knowledge of the fear that this child's mother has to live with in knowing that some in our society do not promise to try and keep her child safe.

I am an empath, one who feels what others feel. I do not know their thoughts in words, only in feelings. I don't read minds. I feel the residue, or the energy, emitted from sadness and sorrow, anger and frustration, hopelessness and depression, and those are but a few examples. I have been known to be driving down the road and peripherally notice a person waiting at the bus stop, only to suddenly be overcome by their sorrow. Or, even more dramatically, to be viewing an exhibit of documents created by our forefathers when, standing before them, I had to hold back a flood of emotions as I was taken by the deep and lingering energetics of their true intentions. Yet, I cannot stop dead in my tracks wherever I am and stop my life as I am overwhelmed by what I feel. Instead, I let it become part of the listening and comprehension that grows within me. It is simply part of the flow of my life, listening and feeling and riding a great tidal wave of information, trusting wherever it may go.

Then I live with a lust for beauty. I live and live and live. Life does not stop in the face of a harsh reality. Those who suffer from depression in a suffocating darkness will tell you that they wish it did, but all of us are witness to the truth that life and all that it entails does go on. However, it is in the quality of this life that we are most challenged. How do we face the turmoil and the tidal-wave effect that confront us during our stay here on earth? For many it is a stormy existence of acting out and aggression. That is the sounding of the alarm that something is terribly wrong and the only escape is to fight a random or elusive battle. For others it is an inevitable caving in or shutting down of self, serving only to repress all that is significant and depressing all hope for a happy and meaningful life. Both scenarios, aggression and depression, are shrouds of trickery, since to shield from life in that way is also to shield from one's self. Escaping from the emptiness in desperation, without awareness of a higher path that is available, becomes the nemesis to a quality of life. It is, indeed, the repulsing of light, for light cannot shine its way through the false bravado of aggressive actions nor the fortress of depression. Love, intimacy, peace, joy, trust, confidence, self-esteem, and spiritual attunement are abandoned under this guise of self-protection. What might have once worked as a child without power no longer works as an adult who has the power of new resources and new awareness?

I can think back to times in my life when I needed protection or safe passage through difficult waters. When a ship sails safely through rocky passageways it must remain safe and intact. I think of those times when I needed to remain safe and whole while sailing or even stalling in stormy seas, times when I had to face myself and my fears, my limits and my perceived weaknesses, where clearly I had to choose whether to sink or swim. Sometimes I wished that someone could just take care of me and relieve me of all responsibility. It is a lesson in becoming "powerful" in oneself, or acquiring personal power, that permits both protection and light to exist together. The quiet power or gentle strength, often originating from the trusted belief that there is more available to us, becomes the resource which allows the bridge to remain open for travel to higher awareness, thus allowing for manifestations of higher functioning for peace of mind and comfort on earth. That inner resource reminds us that we are never alone, always loved, and always prepared for whatever comes our way. All we have to do is put one foot forward and the next will follow. In that way the inner and outer resources, perhaps thought of as the yin and the yang, become one continual flow of dynamics advocating for a more peace-filled life. In becoming powerful one meets the challenges one faces with honesty, integrity, love, and the security that comes from trusting that there is much more. Much more inner strength than ever anticipated, much more light available and accessible, much more guidance and intuitive information, and much more ability to heal or transform as necessary. Self-responsibility, that is, taking care of the self, including mind, body, and spirit, is the arm and the gift of personal power and becomes an express route to spiritual enhancement and renewal. Thus, becoming powerful allows for riding out the storm while trusting that there is an end in sight and, when it's over, there will be a stronger self.

In sharp contrast to becoming powerful, having faith in a power that is only outside of oneself can create a bitter sense of abandonment or falling out of grace (I did something wrong or I must not be worthy), which increases the burden of whatever crisis may be occurring. For example, if one prays to a higher power to help her/him find a job and that does not occur, one can only conclude that she/he was not heard, not cared for, or not worthy. They might not remember to think outside of the box or to use their creativity. Perhaps there were no jobs available in their field, perhaps it was time to learn something new, or change locations; they might have given up their part or their power needed for accomplishing the goal. Hence ensues a further loss of self and feelings of powerlessness and a continued cycle of negativity, resulting in what can be impenetrable grief and lingering depression.

Attending the university in 1971 became another stepping stone. Academic learning was a very small part of the picture at this time, while living away from home out on my own became a springboard for personal study. I was young and often accused of wearing rose-colored glasses or of living in a peaches-and-cream world. That wasn't totally true, but just as I saw the imperfect or flawed reality around me and understood it for what it was, so did I also deeply recognize the potential and possibilities. Thriving on feeling somewhat "limitless" myself, I had not learned how to recognize the boundaries on my areas of influence. I strongly believed in the healing properties of love, and because I could see through the "mask" to the beauty I held fast to my belief in love and its ability to bring about change.

I still believe in the power of love but now understand that it must go hand in hand with self-responsibility. Healing transformation does not occur simply from receiving external love, but must be experienced and felt from the inside out. That is, one must feel worthy of this love and partnership with it in order to create the desired transformation. Love can be a wonderful catalyst for inspirational motivation and change. I felt and deeply believed in the abundance of possibilities available each and every day from which to create a harmonious and balanced life. I continue to feel this way over 35 years later. I've come to realize that I am not just feeling or seeing this potential in some elusive manner. Being an empath, I actually "see" it in the sense of an empathic recognition of the higher self or soul entity, that part of the self that is already functioning at a higher level of awareness and ability. I detect this as the beauty of self in each of us. Improving quality of life requires learning to access the bridge to that higher self, merge with it, and bring it into the realm of daily living.

I feel very fortunate to have the opportunity to witness the beauty, joy, and serenity that is always there, sometimes seeming to lurk beneath the surface but always there and alluding to potential and possibilities. It is like looking in a muddy pool and watching as it clears. In particular, in witnessing this miraculous metamorphosis with clients who, through our hypnotic sessions, had touched this sacred place within, at least for a moment, I sometimes took for granted that they were now ready to maintain this transition. Sometimes they simply responded to the reflection of my vision of them but did not truly experience this enough for themselves. Only when one can truly connect or relate to this vision and conceive that, yes, there is a higher self, can healing transformation then begin. I have learned that this cannot be forced and in many ways this is a comfort to me. I no longer feel responsible for everyone else's miracles, only for my own!

One goes through life to find or rediscover wisdom and truth. In my early twenties, not holding as much clarity as I do now, my quest to heal (referring to mind, body, and spirit) with love also became my thirst to find the right love. So in this awkward way, sometimes choosing to shy from self and sometimes unwittingly giving self away, a journey towards a deepening of self continued.

Without knowing it for what it was, a thread of guidance remained true and on course, and I followed where it led. Of course, there is no misguided action or going astray which is not included in the awakening of self. It must all be there and accepted for what it is and loved for its part. It is part of the picture, and as the picture develops, trust is strengthened in the recognition that each pearl (misshapen or not) is a part of the strand, and so it flows.

I Am The Quiet Of The Falling Snow

Let The River Flow

Let the river flow, I say
No dam is strong enough to hold.
The inner and the outer rings
Innately carve a path twofold
for each a private will to hold.
The river winds and turns and bends its way
but never lets direction stray.

So let the river flow, I say
no dam is strong enough to hold.
For each is what they are today
and for this moment that shall remain.
Yet change is not denied its day
what once was here may change its way.
So let the river flow, I say
For certainly it knows the way.

1990

$\mathcal{H}$ ONORING THE FLOW

We live in a society that promotes separation and specialization. Many view their life's experiences as isolated and sometimes random events. When two things do appear to interact or show synchronicity they are often dismissed as mere coincidences. The lack of intersection and connection between things represents umbrella symptoms reflected in a society that plays host to many manifestations of disrespect to life. That, along with easily available, high-tech living, makes it very easy for humankind to feel separate from the natural world, and this helps to rationalize reckless manipulation and control. Humans seem to thrive on this false sense of power. This often rash and shortsighted control permeates all levels of life down to the innermost core of existence. All feelings of trust and awe about this truly miraculous life that consists of intricately woven relationships are forgotten.

I can remember going camping with a friend in the early 80s. I was living in Oregon at the time in a double-wide trailer surrounded by mint fields. It was November, right around Thanksgiving, and my friend was coming for a visit. He expected a lovely camping trip to be planned in one of Oregon's wintergreen wood-lands. It was always green in the winter because of the heavy rainfall, and this made for enchanting wilderness experiences. Of course, in winter at the higher elevations it was also cold, snowy, and icy.

Being somewhat of a novice at planning these trips I chose a spot out by the McKenzie River with which I was somewhat familiar. I grabbed my down sleeping bag that had a broken zipper, packed an assortment of easy foods, and we jumped into my yellow Volkswagen Thing, which was truly a very lightweight car pretending to be a jeep. Though a somewhat hesitant driver, I took the driver's seat and drove us to our destination. Arriving was not an easy task as the access road was very, very icy! Still unhampered and non-panicked, I drove us through to our campsite. Feeling rather proud of myself and comfortable that I had done my part, we unloaded the car and made camp. I was prepared for a delightful time. The next day we emerged from the tent, greeted the cold day, and began our exploration of the woods. Then it happened: our energies collided. I watched with horror as my companion came upon a winter deciduous tree, barren and presumed dead. He threw his arms around the tree, not in an embrace, but in a dramatic display of confrontation. He then began to rock back and forth, carrying the tree further and further back each time in his determination to jostle and bring the tree down. I was outraged! What utter arrogance and absolute disregard for that tree's right to stand there in the woods with dignity until it was its time to fall. My friend was not planning to use the wood for fuel, nor had he any plans to build a structure. He gave no thought to what other beings he may have dislodged or interrupted. He was simply making sport out of the activity. Standing outside of the circle enables one to dishonor and forget about the gentle balance which maintains the strength of the circle and the integrity of an ecosystem. I wondered why he gave no thought to the life which was supported by the tree simply because it was still standing there.

An existence of simply being and remaining valuable regardless of obvious worth is an ideal that seems to fly above many human values. Therefore, my friend chose to approach the tree as a foe and challenged its right to stand. Perhaps he felt exuberant with power as he watched the tree fall. I do not know. I did not ask him. I instead was struck speechless at this thoughtless act of unkindness.

The Cardinal

I am grateful for the cardinal that sits upon the dead tree branches.
The highest point is where he can be seen,
delicately balanced and singing a persistent cord.

Naked tree branches extend out towards the sun.
A chilling wind has made them frail and brittle appendages no longer
serving for the continuance of life.

Now, a tree no longer capable of nourishing
its own splintered structure,
yet a cardinal sits upon the dead tree branches and glows red against
the sun's amber rays.
There is dignity after life.

1986

I continue to think about such exuberant expressions of power and control. Perhaps this ability to conquer becomes an archetype for behavior, or perhaps it reflects a long history of an archetype deeply ingrained within the human psyche. We can, therefore we do. This ability to manipulate nature has widespread consequences, especially when done with so little forethought and awareness. In this way it can be very counter to our intuitive wisdom, so it may be a style of living that keeps us from ourselves and blocks us from what is truly for the highest good of all concerned. It is said that as human beings we have the gifts of intellect for problem solving and a physical body for strength and for the fine motor skills needed to navigate the intricacies that we come upon in life. When used in wholeness or whole self with heart and spirit, we can enhance the opportunity for a superb life for all beings on earth.

However, if we remain aloof from the web of life we stand the chance of maintaining a narrow and shortsighted life. We all know the anecdote of the child who plays with tools without guidance and becomes a danger to him/herself and others. So it is that we find our world on a collision course with our very lifeline, our mother Earth. This is not new or surprising information. The reports are constant. There are global warming and environmental disasters, increasing violence with our children being violent towards each other, rainforest depletion, and wildlife extinction. It can sound and feel very depressing. Even within this guise of separateness, there can be no doubt but that we are all profoundly affected by such actions, and on some level we understand the irony of our circumstance. It is then natural to overcompensate insidiously for this loss of spiritual identity on earth since we no longer consciously remember having the experience of the sublime freedom that occurs in a non-physical reality. In the absent-minded longing for what has been lost and has become unknown, one can take comfort in a concrete ability to control. It appears to me that this issue of power and control becomes very confused. For instance, when it comes to believing in oneself and remaining in a personal relationship with the higher self, so many people give this away and defer to a worshiping system or structure that is solely outside of themselves. Many succumb to what is said to be a higher authority. The inner authority, the higher self, is often neglected and hence we lose personal power and control. Sometimes unknowingly and at subtle levels, this becomes demeaning and undermining to a good self-esteem, and leads to feeling powerless and out of control. So it is easy to compensate for this by becoming engrossed in other means of control, which furthers the disassociation from the larger and more whole picture. This is unfortunate, because it is so beneficial to remember that there is so much more to each of our stories than we might know at the moment on hand, and this larger knowledge is a huge reservoir of personal resource just waiting to be of service.

It is common to remain stuck in the premature gratification received from false control. Who hasn't been down this road many times? I continue to look for the balance between actively manipulating to manifest a dream, and simply relaxing and maintaining a thoughtful intention and then allowing the river to flow. This is no easy task. With all the talk about "creating your own reality" and manifesting what is desired in life, this can become a confusing point. Just what does it mean to create reality? Is it a matter of force and will power, or clarity of mind and presence of being? Is it a matter of prejudging all unforeseen circumstances while anticipating and preparing for this unknown? Or is there a time when we trust and simply let the river flow? Most likely this riddle is not solved by either approach but by an expanded awareness or mindfulness that allows for balancing all of the above as needed. Again, as with the yin and the yang, there cannot be shadow without the sunshine.

Forked Path Riddle

The nightingale sang out in jest
with full moon standing by,
hey ho
down there ye travelers
for which path shall you try?

I'll ask the night wind, and I the star,
and I the moon in full.
And so they traveled to and fro
and hoped to solve the riddle.

And now the night was growing dim
the moon set down in style
and nightingale joined by a coyote
did laugh and clown in style.

How shall I find the answer?
I do not know the way.
My mind is drawn to the light of the east
and my inner heart to the westward day.

At just that moment the sky did break
and the earth began to shake.
The path did twist and turn away
and wiggled off as a wise old snake.

1981

S HEDDING THE OLD Skin

Shedding the old skin begins in the form of a pure and honest intention to do so, as well as clear motivations and the desire to walk a true path with heart. This involves soul searching and a willingness to face oneself honestly and lovingly even in the darkest moments. When maintaining this self-love and releasing self- degradation, this path becomes much less threatening both in concept and in process. Who cannot think of a time, when deep in conversation, that they might grow increasingly attached and opinionated in direct correlation to the amount of opposition they were receiving, while at the same time knowing this to be true but feeling too threatened to admit it and possibly expose a *fault* or *weakness*? It is much easier to set the ego free when it is understood that this issue of being correct or "right" is not linked to personal worth or worthiness. We are all worthy at all times-- worthy of receiving love and worthy of giving love--exactly as we are every step along the way of this evolving journey.

Daring to dream back to other times, I find memories of conflicts, traumas, misspoken words, betrayals, rejections and such. It would not be an earth-time existence without the intermingling of these events, and so it is not difficult to see that the skin can grow very thick. In fact, for many it seems that this is what life is about. It is not uncommon to hear that one must be "toughened up" and prepared to live in the real world. Childhood seems to get shorter as we hasten to introduce our children to this world. The natural lightness that is born within and connects us to the beyond, and which by right should be preserved, is instead made heavy.

Each of us, when we are ready, may decide to face this challenge and reclaim this lightness that is rightfully ours. Unconditional love, beauty, intimacy, peace, self-respect and integrity of being, spiritual enhancement, and joy are just some of the light available to be re-found and re-traced into being. I think of this as the new fabric of the vital self as one by one these fibers of light are strengthened and re-woven into an energy that can then manifest as an entity with quality of life. This job of shedding the old skin is not done quickly and will not be attempted by anyone who is impatient or unwilling to put forth a tremendous effort.

Our dear friends of the reptilian nature do not shed their skins easily or without a price to pay. Snakes, for example, alternately soak in water, scrape against rock, and remain very still. They do not take sustenance throughout this time. Only the bare essentials are tended to, as vision becomes cloudy while the old skin now covers the eyes. One can only speculate as to whether they experience a sense of vulnerability at this time, but at last the breakthrough occurs. The shedding has been accomplished and replaced as new, radiant skin now sparkling with rainbow light emerges. Renewed, it is understood to be the time to move on and continue with life. The human Zen of shedding old skin is certainly quite different from this. For snakes it is a very natural process which is not feared. Humans are not cool or detached by nature and will cling to the security of what is known, often at all cost. So it is not surprising that for some, personal vision can remain in a clouded state long after the time to "shed" has passed over and over again. Old information and preconceived ideas and concepts about life and what it was supposed to be all take refuge within the deep crevices of fear. Fear of the unknown is frequently reinforced throughout life and regularly becomes viewed as a dreaded destination. Even depression and paralyzing anxiety can take preference over venturing out into unknown terrain. I am reminded of a story told in *Seven Arrows*, by Hyemeyohsts Storm, called "Jumping

Mouse." The story tells of a mouse who truly marches to a different drummer. Jumping Mouse is sure that there is much more to life than that which meets the eye. Though just a young mouse and ridiculed for his efforts, Jumping Mouse trusts in what he "knows" to be true and chooses a path that leads him to the sacred mountains which he sought. It was a difficult and perilous journey, but Jumping Mouse holds true to this path and is greatly rewarded. Like Jumping Mouse, once the journey begins we cannot always know what we will encounter along the way. It is a brilliant display of trust and true spiritual relationship when one actively commits to this unknown destination. It reflects an immense and profound statement of faith to say, " I am prepared for this journey because I am guided, I trust myself, and I will know what to do every step along the way. Ho! And so it shall be."

Unknown Destination

I imagine an hourglass filled with sand slowly flowing.
Grain by grain, changing the structure and unfolding
the story of an unknown destination.

I see rotating doors reflecting the comings and goings
through phases of life.
An accelerated pace, then painfully slow,
and sometimes... a stop.

I hear music playing an array of questions and answers,
with harmonic intonations implying a response
left open for interpretation.

I feel the tantalizing movements of the Chinese shadowbox.
Intervals of movement and pause,
a chime's voice adds coordination and prediction.

I taste the dancer's intuitive flavor.
A burst of energy guided by dramatic balance.
Motion flowing in symbiotic cooperation,
controlled and responsive.

I smell the fire burning within
as I sort through the chambers of unexplored knowledge.
Looking for clues and messages,
and mapping out libraries for future reference.

I imagine an hourglass filled with sand that goes on forever,
easily flowing and softly unfolding the story
of an unknown destination.

1985

$\mathcal{U}$NKNOWN DESTINATION

Releasing that which is no longer a benefit is truly a lightening of the load. Much of what we carry with us serves only to dig the groove of old habits deeper and deeper, making them heavier and heavier. To unload these past weights requires an introspective look at habits and patterns in life. So much of who we are is a combination of socialization from family and institutions, as well as the karmic package with which we arrived. Our thinking process, how we communicate, interests, work, point of view, relationship style, and overall style of life are so often adopted without conscious awareness and adapted to as if there were no choice.

My father and I used to engage in debates regarding the question concerning humans and free will. My father was certain that humans did not have free will. He felt that this was evidenced by the degenerating state of the world. He asserted that humans had an innate nature and that it was obvious that no amount of effort could or would change this. This conversation was very sad for me, because I knew that these thoughts reflected his circumstances and his inability to change his own life. Though a brilliant and sensitive man, he lacked the stamina of inspiration required for keeping hope and trust in his heart.

I, on the other hand, have always been an idealist through and through, strongly believing in the human spirit and its ability to persevere and create beneficial change. It's not surprising that I have been guided to work in the world using the tools of a hypnotherapist for promoting and encouraging this attribute of healthy change. As adamantly as my father denied free will, I proclaimed it and all the potential it afforded. Certainly as individuals we have predispositions and tendencies which could be astrologically, sociologically, genetically, and/or karmically imposed--probably all of the above! None, however, are written in stone, and all can be transformed through expanded awareness, personal/spiritual growth, and the intention to do so.

This, of course, is the ideal and not easily achieved, but who said it had to be easy? It is not a bad destination to have in mind and to aspire to. Clearly, that very aspiration is the first breath that leads to the light which leads us out of the tunnel. Our society reflects an abundance of tunnel vision, resulting in a narrowing of perceptions about choices in life. A lack of mindfulness, or fully living and being present in each moment, can keep us stuck in patterns of creating life through non-choices and maintaining the status quo. In essence we end up with the leftovers! So in not living life with some understanding of self which allows for some clarity of intention, we end up maintaining a life of sameness, for better or for worse. No change, no growth, and no challenge. Even if our human aspect will settle for this, our soul aspect will not. Instead, we receive wake-up calls presented in many creative ways. Difficulty in relationships and communication, loneliness, depression, anxiety, boredom, being accident-prone, disharmony, and illness can be manifestations of our soul or higher self-urging us to wake up. When life no longer holds enchantment for you it may be time to take the challenge and accept the call. This then becomes a journey towards enlightened living while facing these challenges, discovering new opportunities and feeling alive along the way. Sometimes emotions and feelings of anguish break their way to the surface and demand to be acknowledged and then released. This is not always a Prozac moment! This process can be supported by the light of love and compassion, which among other things serves to resuscitate our connection with our higher self and becomes the link or bridge to the infinite source of all that is (God, Buddha, Great Spirit, chi field, etc.). This connection, which can show itself through synchronicities in living, reminds us that we are never alone, which in itself brings great comfort and can help to release the struggles throughout the journey. Taking the first step of questioning one's purpose for being here, while opening personal awareness to your own true self, becomes the initial fuel needed for creating a new and more satisfying perpetual motion.

After some time, and seemingly with much less effort, this positive motion will take on a life of its own, helping to manifest that which is for your highest good. It is good to note that this motion does not have to be spring-loaded and experienced in leaps and bounds. Each of us has our own personal time clock that measures readiness, so we can be paced according to our own abilities to absorb and utilize new information. There is beauty found in remembering that the preliminary energy or footsteps put forth towards unknown terrain are the most difficult steps to be taken. Thereafter, as with everything else in life, it gets easier. Practice truly is worth its weight in gold, or in this case, in light and inspiration. There is no greater gift than to be inspired about life. This does not necessarily curtail hardship. Just knowing that there are children suffering anywhere on the planet creates a hardship for our sensitivities. However, inspiration and trust help to remind us that there is so much more than what we perceive at this time, and that each of us is so much more than an accumulation of our experiences here on earth.

So, as the gears are greased and awareness begins to shift, a new positive and exciting cycle of exploration begins to take over and carries a momentum of its own! In this way the old vicious cycle is broken and left to atrophy from neglect. As this occurs one's life is blessed in turn, with delightful "coincidences" that in themselves further this new awakening. Suddenly the mysterious flavor of the unknown in regards to those things, which can be felt and not seen, rekindles the appetite and re-focuses our vision to notice the miracles in life. As we build this bridge of higher understanding that allows spirit guidance to be with us everyday, we are not diminishing its majesty. It could be said that this is in truth the beginning of bringing heaven to earth. Though this sojourn remains open and with no end in sight, a subtle metamorphosis has occurred as the dreaded unknown destination is no longer dreaded.

Light As A Feather

Motion, the motion of my spirit
gliding through space.
Frothy and free and light,
light as a feather.

And my mind zig-zags through eternity and time,
slippery and elusive.
A juggling act between them and me.

Evolution, the evolution of my mind
chasing my spirit through space,
metamorphosing into a butterfly.

Freedom in flight.
The balance in life precarious.
Light as a feather.

1981

$\mathcal{L}$ IGHT AS A Feather

As we begin to challenge old belief systems, which probably were not really chosen with awareness in the first place, and we begin to explore other ways of living in this earth-time reality, we may find that these challenges lead to questions about the very nature of what we once held to be the "truth" about our reality. This could be the beginning of the opening of the ever famous Pandora's Box. Once the dust dissipates and the air is cleared around us, this old abandoned treasure could lead to new levels of personal knowing, expanded understanding, and a stronger sense of trust that could potentially permeate all the way to the core of our being.

Some may fear the experience of opening this mythical box filled with new ideas and possibilities and think it will lead them astray or overwhelm them with temptation. However, to look at it from another point of view, one might find it expansive, truly liberating. In fact, it may even be the key for removing the chains that have kept most of us stuck in illusions about ourselves and the possibilities, which exist for us. Once the box is opened the light has the opportunity to illuminate those things which have not been noticed before, like rummaging through a long forgotten chest packed securely and left to be rediscovered at some future date just precisely when needed the most. As something new is gained so, too, an old layer is peeled and left behind to lighten the load, and in this way old burdens are cast away.

Great relief is born out of the discarding of that which no longer "fits." The heavy weights are cast out and the jewels are permitted in.

Putting words on paper awakens memories as one string of thought can lead to another, and so it is for me at this time. It seems that moments of crisis and despair are not hard to retrieve when I glance back to 1983. Tim and I had been happily married for one year and committed to our life together. We were living in a very rustic shanty. Though it did have running water and indoor plumbing, the latter was generally found in the most unusual places. Our guests were amused to find the bathroom facilities and the shower in opposite corners of the kitchen and the bathtub eloquently placed in the greenhouse. Of course, for us that only added to its charm. The greenhouse was home to grapefruit, mandarin orange, and avocado trees, along with an assortment of geraniums, begonias, and my dearest African violets. Topping it off were the irresistible tree frogs that took residence there and sang harmoniously to us throughout our stay. We had very nice gardens filled with beds of snow peas and greens, squash and beans, daylilies and strawberry patches, and carrots often needed to be dug out of muddy rain puddles.

Included in this Eden of wonders were the sorrows: miscarriages, financial woes, career disappointments and, worst of all, the sudden death of my dear friend, Phil, who had so ruffled my feathers years earlier by knocking over dead trees. This time, I'm afraid, it was he who could not stand up to the force of Mother Nature as he was overcome and buried by an avalanche. I carried much grief that year. Phil, my sister's brother-in-law, was from Michigan, as was I. I could not make it back from Oregon for the funeral and felt very lonely as I tried to honor his life and go through my grief. Tim, sadly, had not met Phil, so although he supported my loss, it was not his loss. It was difficult to feel present in life, and I often felt like I was in some distant and very thick fog. I am not sure that it would ever have cleared had it not been for the countless hours I spent in my two healing chambers, the greenhouse and my garden. They each became places of sacred solitude and quiet where the trickling rays of light were patiently seeking re-entry into my heart.

The way in which we perceive our reality changes many times in a single lifespan, and once again my reality eventually began to grow lighter. There is much to be gained from these periods of introspection and healing that gently allow for the processing of new information. Our perspective is challenged even as existence can seem precarious and fragile. As we come to terms with loss it must be understood that nothing will ever be the same again. It may look the same on the outside, but deep inside there has been growth and change which feeds a new understanding.

Years later I had several opportunities to speak at a bereavement center created in particular for children who had experienced losses. I usually spoke to the volunteers who were facilitating support groups for those children who had either lost a loved one or were themselves facing life-threatening illnesses. I discussed the value of relaxation, stillness, quiet, and the use of skills such as visualization and hypnosis for accessing an expanded awareness and a new understanding about both life and death transitions, as well as for offering comfort, peace of mind, and hopefulness. This understanding is already within us, at least in our higher selves, and can be utilized throughout our lives for comfort and guidance. I was once asked a precious question by my own daughter, only four or five at the time, who, having lost her cherished grandfather, was told that in time she would feel better. " Why Mama, why will time make me feel better?" To many it may seem that she was given the trite and common response to her grief. However, time truly does allow for the possibility of healing through new and higher understanding, especially if one uses their time well. This "new understanding" or shift in perspective can assist in the evolution of the human experience by transforming a heavy heart into the lightness of a feather that will someday return to eagle.

Eagle Dance

A mountain top high enough to feel the great spirit's heartbeat.
Drums pursuing ancient tongues.
Hey ye hey ye hey ye hey ye.
Softly fading prayers honoring the eagle,
the winged beings who soar to other worlds.

We offer you this prayer
and in your honor we dance to the four directions.
Hey ye hey ye hey ye hey ye.
Drums louder and louder, each note as if in a dream,
like water dropping, bouncing, changing shape.
Changing time. Great capes of feathers swirling and daring,
stirring up dust from the earth mother.
Dust and smoke becoming a ghost messenger to the great spirit.

We seek a vision.
Let us cling to the wings of the great eagle
and see through the eyes of longsighted wisdom.
Grandfather eagle, grandmother eagle,
in your honor we walk in peace.

1985

$\mathcal{P}$RAYING WITH EAGLE

As feather returns to eagle, so do I look to spirit for guidance and healing? This higher and inner source of information offers solace in times of grief, and inspiration at times when hope is lost or at least hidden from view.

These thoughts return me to the early 80's when I began to participate in Home Hospice Care. This was when I was still living in Oregon and Hospice was still a grassroots effort. My contribution was to offer Hypnotherapy and Therapeutic Touch as a means for enhancing well being, comfort, and healing on whatever level was possible. Hypnosis served as the link for connecting to the subconscious and cellular level, as well as being a bridge which could facilitate reconnecting or merging with the higher self. When combining this altered state with energy work the benefits were greatly compounded, resulting in extreme serenity and receptivity to new realities. Cells were asked to rejuvenate and restore their particular areas in the body, while the subconscious mind could then communicate to the entire body that this was occurring, promoting a unified and focused mind/body/spirit intention. Strong suggestions for comfort, relief, well-being, and healing transformation were imprinted at the cellular level along with the hopefulness that this would manifest in a way that was best for the individual. This worked beautifully for pain management and also for maintaining personal power and integrity during what was often a time of transitioning into death and beyond.

I am flooded with memories of Serena, a beautiful young girl of eleven years. Serena demonstrated an eagerness to learn techniques that would help her to continue her normal activities for as long as possible. This meant that she would have to learn to manage her headaches and stomach pain, which interfered both with her dancing, that she loved, and her overall attendance at school. Driven by her adolescent wish to achieve normalcy in her life, Serena easily embraced relaxation tools and the use of her own hands as instruments for relief and comfort. It was a moving and thrilling experience to witness her expansion in this way. There were many shifts of awareness that Serena had to make over the months, including conquering many fears. I had the honor of being with her when, after a prolonged absence from school, she demanded the opportunity to go to school and face her peers. I knew that in truth she was now ready to face herself and her pending transition. Serena wanted to say good-bye, which she did with eloquence and dignity. At the tender age of 12, Serena died a warrioress's death as a whole person and on her terms. I am still very moved each time I think of her.

It is very difficult to maintain the feeling of being a competent and valuable human being while experiencing a chronic or degenerating and sometimes life-threatening illness. Decisions begin being made for you in an attempt to "help you," which often results in the encroaching illness' ability to take over and become you. At this point the individual is often ignored and the "patient" is simply perceived as "the illness." This is a very insidious and grave loss which interferes with the healing process of transition. Healing can become a confusing issue, for the human and earthly understanding of what healing means may be different from the spiritual knowledge of what is healing and necessary at any given time. This is probably one of the hardest conclusions to swallow. Those of us who wish to be healed on earth generally wish to remain on earth as well! That is not always how it works. For those whose life journey involves facilitating the healing process it could easily feel as though we sometimes come up against this wall. We then determine whether we can surrender to it or vanquish with despair.

I have experienced both emotions. Surrendering requires a tremendous amount of trust and letting go of what we think we know, which is not easy to come by. Praying with Eagle has always helped me. Commonly, praying is external. We ask for help, that is, outside of ourselves, to change a situation or an outcome. If that happens, then all is well and faith is renewed; that is a good start. However, if the reversal does not occur there is often bewilderment, extreme loneliness, and discouragement. We can feel that there is no place else to turn. Praying with Eagle is my metaphor, symbolically representing the co-creative process that occurs when we agree to a partnership between ourselves and spirit so that we are an active participant in the desired manifestation, consciously supporting the desired outcome while also acknowledging that there are unknown factors which could be out of our domain of influence.

There are times when it may be necessary for a re-evaluation of current circumstances and the willingness to change that "reality," or perceptions of that reality, as needed. Willingness is a key component here. Participating as a co-creator will always include an expanded awareness of *self* and a deeper spiritual relationship. For awareness of *self* brings us closer to living in alignment with our soul self, which in turn closes the gap between us and the larger collective body of spirit (God, Great Spirit, etc.). The journey toward *self* becomes an introspective study which is found in stillness. Praying with Eagle becomes the creative force behind the inspiration that moves us to take a leap into unknown terrain. Surrendering does not mean to simply give up. It means accepting that outcome remains unknown to us. It means remembering that guidance and divine intervention come in all kinds of shapes and forms. Sometimes they appear in the form of clarity and courage, assisting us to truly step out of our old fears so we can prepare to face a new day filled with opportunities for continued transformation available and accessible for us. I have been fortunate enough to bear witness to many who have gracefully embraced their transition into death with beauty, courage, and dignity. In those moments all time stood still, and the concept of surrendering became crystallized for me.

So, Praying with Eagle involves clear intentions and affirmation of these intentions on a daily basis. In effect, there is not a day that goes by where we are not reminded of our unique purpose and journey here and of the subtle shifts that continue to occur within. Those little glimpses here and there of new abilities and new insights, new strengths and increased determination, all often leading to new opportunities, will lend light to a new and ever changing picture of *self*. Therefore, an exciting re-imaging of one's *self* takes place and one begins to understand that yes, this is a never ending journey, and that is "the good news."

Living Manifestations

Manifestations,
Dreams into light
Images growing
Taking form in this life.

Realities shifting
Day into night,
Thought forms affirming
This powerful sight.

Dreamtime,
The heart's mind
Transcending this earthtime
Creating...enhancing...
Embodying this lifetime.

Manifestations,
Dreams into light
Creating the day...
Directing the night.

1990

$\mathcal{L}$ IVING MANIFESTATIONS

Have you ever stood before a mirror and really studied your reflection? Noticing the contour of your face, acknowledging every line and wrinkle, the shape of your lips and the way that your cheekbones support your face. Next, allowing yourself to become captivated by your own eyes filled with the richness of ancestral callings and tomorrows yearnings. Then suddenly you experience a great wave of distancing and detachment. For just a moment all sense of recognition and personal identity has left you, gone into a shadowy past. Possibly you will see mother, father, grandmother or grandfather staring back at you. In this split second of shifting reality you have come face to face with eternity.

This experience, both sobering and sensational, becomes more so as you place your hands on both sides of your face and lovingly cradle this *self*. This soul self, familiar and strange, invites recognition for lessons learned and journeys taken together all for your benefit, because you are significant and in the vast hugeness and wholeness of eternity you still matter. Isn't that awe inspiring? That one grain of sand on the beach, out of millions, is meaningful. In the hustle and bustle of life on earth this preciousness is often lost in the shuffle. The clock is ticking, the meter is running, and we are off and running, but keeping sight of meaning and spiritual significance is one contest that must not be lost, for this is a contest of a lifetime. Can we live on Earth and meet this challenge to retain focus and internal awareness? Can we live the duality of soaring with the angels while our feet are still planted firmly on the earth, giving us the ability to be nourished in every step and to also anchor heaven's (chi, love and compassion) light for us to use here on Earth.

For myself, in my daily life I enjoy a trail of manifestations left by my intentions, as they are actualized and now available to me. A trail of light manifested in the expression of children and loving relationships, poetry and gardens, art and beauty, animals and oneness with all beings, and gentle living on our Mother Earth. Living as a scout on this trail demands fully committing to self-responsibility and the sensitive use of power for the highest good. For some, just the words, "self-responsibility," leaves a sting or bitter aftertaste. For me, by contrast, I taste the satisfaction of personal integrity and wholeness. I look forward to flying with Eagle across all boundaries and bridging the gap between the inner and outer realms of understanding, and in this way discovering my direction in life and thus trusting that this direction will always take me home to *self.* There is no longer a need for confusion about who did what and why. There is no confusion about who I am and what path has brought me to this point.

I come into contact with many people who are going through changes in their lives, frequently a change in a relationship. Those times are, of course, very trying. What makes it worse is when it is compounded by the fact that many have not been their own pilot for a very long time. Having lived the life of unclear intentions where someone else often, and sometimes routinely, made the decisions and acted as the navigator, a separation can lead to a strong loss of identity or an identity crisis. Many who had hoped they would be at the time of their life where they were grounded and rooted in security are now instead faced with being out on their own and asking that ancient question, "Who am I and how in the world did I get to this point?" Those are good questions, and surprisingly they can be answered.

Traveling this road to inner discoveries might not have been the first choice on the agenda but it will turn out to be the most enlightening, and if permitted to, it will take those who choose to walk the path, far beyond what might have been possible for them in the old reality. Much gets left behind, given away, or lost when identity and *self* are packaged neatly and given over to another's control. It is healing to the soul to go back, re-group, and reclaim those pieces of beauty that were slowly and blindly discarded over time.

That Which Is The Beauty

She wandered around aimlessly amongst the weeping willows,
And she was weeping too. Only you couldn't see the tears.

She wasn't quite invisible, not really.
Her veils were transparent, but you couldn't see her tears, not really.

But, I knew that she wept. I saw it in her form.
A surreal image projected through the mist.
A frail frame bent towards looking for what isn't,
and missing that which is.

That which is the beauty of the woman that she is.
She wasn't quite invisible, not really.
Her isolation was translucent, but you couldn't see the tears,
not really.

But I knew that she wept, I saw it in her gaze.
A distant glance at nothing, a frozen glare at pain.
A distant glance at nothing, she said she didn't see.
A frozen glare at pain, she said she didn't feel.
She wasn't quite invisible, not really.
Her face was like a journal disclosing many days.
Many days of wandering amongst the weeping willows.

She was weeping too, and now I saw the tears.
Rivers joyously cascading and releasing all her fears.

Many years have come and gone, and she has found her way.
Re-stepping all her footsteps and what was missed
throughout those days,
while looking for what isn't and missing that which is.
That which is the beauty of the woman that she is.

1985

$\mathcal{T}$ HAT WHICH IS the Beauty

I love to think about the whole conception and preconception time of life. This miraculous junction where spirit and soul truly materialize before our eyes. Just think of it! An egg seed, sperm, and spirit are married. Then, with the passing of time, voilà, baby life emerges, carrying within itself the answers to all of its questions along with the potential for all possibilities and the eternity of universal knowledge, packed away small enough to keep safe and sound to form its own microscopic version of the *big story*. That wisdom all sown up and threaded so finely throughout their fabric that they may never know that it is there. During pre-conception reality, a woman's bodily wisdom uses that embedded information, which is delicately interpreted to prepare her body for new life. All this as though it were simply routine, and so we think it is. It's easy to think of it as solely mechanics. The brain computer prepares programs throughout the body with precision for hormonal cycles, preparation of the uterus, release of the egg, and fertilization, all orchestrated like a master clockworks. Though this in itself is impressive enough, I prefer to remember the union that occurred between realities. Here for the purpose of birth and renewal, lessons to be learned and universal continuity and expansion, spirit manifests on earth and graces this earthbound existence by uplifting and embodying each of us with all that is needed.

Hence, with love and willingness, spirit descends to Earth and lives the illusion of the physical, and so we are born. I suppose that my earthly quest has always been to narrow the distance between these realities and to clearly *know* my spirit self while living here on Earth. I want to lift the curtain, see behind the illusions, and then vow to never be fooled by this trick again, for to be fooled is to lose that which was given to us to be held safe. It is my intention each day to retrace the steps of old disguises, to sweep up the remains of preconceived ideas that are the leftovers of old ghosts, which then became thoughts and words and undesirable manifestations. To do this, each day must be remembered to be and received as a new day. Acknowledging it as a good day to be alive and to greet with affection all of the gifts that are within and holding the potential to be realized. What are these gifts if they are not the potential to know our own beauty? To know our beauty is to live our life in a beautiful way, which in essence is to focus our highest awareness for the purpose of anchoring the purest white light of love here to stay on Earth as a guiding force. In this way we allow for new perceptions, new abilities, and new awakenings in each moment. Thus, new beginnings and opportunities for transformation are available everyday. These new beginnings can be seen as the rebirths and new conceptions of *self*. Again, a rendezvous with spirit while here on Earth, for each time we rise to the occasion for this expansion of *self*, the divinity of spirit becomes more accessible. Now with the assistance of these "spirit helpers" (our higher self, guides, angels, etc.) we can live more in alignment with our soul's intent. The help has always been there, just gently waiting for us to see beyond our nose! Just waiting for our senses to heighten and our minds to clear so we can become more acutely aware and ready to receive. That is, we can begin to experience a more multi-dimensional reality. This continues to create shifts in our thinking and in the ability to use our senses more fully. Suddenly the quiet is not just the lack of sound to our ears but is instead felt in the mind and the body as stillness ensues. Listening now becomes a blending of this new sensual continuum as information stirs and re-sounds in our innermost caverns. This listening becomes a grandiose moment of euphoric receptivity harmonized for perfect and complete understanding.

I can think of many occasions when I entered this state of *harmonic listening* and truly became one with my surroundings. For me this often involved a joining with the tree beings, with roots firmly planted in the Earth our mother and branches swaying in the breeze with a gentle and graceful agility. Soon my own arms held the grace from this gentle being, while my legs remained balanced and flexible, sharing the strength of these magnificent tree beings. During these moments all else stops, the mind quiets, and peace flows like tiny rivulets guided in their direction home. These are beautiful and wondrous moments! There were times I wanted to shout for joy, stopped only by the preciousness of the silence.

Other times I would feel the need to weep welling up inside, due also to the joy from this lovely recognition of belonging. All expectations and critical judgments are subdued by the sacred communion with life. Gratefully, during these excursions there is no room for the trivial or petty thinking which can be associated with life on Earth. That is forgotten and left behind. All that remains is the supreme contentment that comes from being so connected. In these moments, which surpass all others, the shroud of separateness is removed, old longings are dismissed, and great love emerges in their place.

Weaver's Story

She sat cross-legged and straight. Her back supported
only by habit and resolve.
A shawl loosely folded around her shoulders, promising relief,
born only in faith
that it would provide the necessary warmth and comfort
throughout the cool fall evening.

Her face was still. Wrinkles winding pathways around its surface.
Some lines were new and light,
barely claiming residence to the spot they occupied.
Others were deep and grooved, carved into permanence
by a sculptor's harsh hand and a relentless sun.
Still others were worn and faded,
indifferent to the story that once marked their birth.
Now scrubbed and erased, no longer a scar,
and yet the memory remains.

Her hands were strong and patient.
Slowly and precisely guiding the layers of dried grass and vine.
The light, now dim as the sun lowered in the sky,
did not disturb her rhythm.
Fingers once timid and unsure, now easily sensed their
direction and gracefully laced the twine,
row after row, around the universe that was hers.
Her eyes were not vacant, they were deep.
Her stillness hid the symphony with which her prayers danced.
It was never the same. Sometimes a monotone low and intense,
and sometimes a climax of discovery and decision.
Often a lullaby secure and reassuring
offering communication of love and tenderness.

She followed the path of the sunset and slowly stopped her work.
Her eyes caught the colors that painted the sky,
as she silently blessed the mother and caressed the earth.

1985

S TORY EMERGES

Slowly, patiently does story emerge. Over time and space the river meanders in and out of little crevices of life, picking up experiences, traveling through reactions and outcomes, or perhaps branching off along a different fork in an attempt to learn new lessons or to run from old lessons still waiting for completion. The river, through osmosis, collects the rich remains of fertile and textured soil. It carries the reflections of water found in crystal droplets from medicine lakes as well as the muddy waters which have not yet cleared from the passing storm.

Story emerges in the poetry of everyday living. It will emerge where there is awareness and where there is not. For always, with the passage of time, there is story. Decisions made or not become scripted in the play. Some may think that River travels to the ocean randomly finding her way. That is not so. Watch as River makes her way around bends and snakes her way between inlets, weaving through land and cities, and sniffing her way through a path of least resistance. Never does she choose a path that leads upstream. River flows with the challenge of journeying home and sets her course with empowerment and clarity. She knows her priorities, where she is going, and where she has come from.

Story emerges. Seasons come and go, and some memories fade with their colors washed and dulled by many rains. Still, River grows ripe and confident. She has gathered many treasures along her trek, and a natural automatic wisdom now guides her through the thick and thin of her story.

No longer burdened with questions and long replies, River now flows with the grace of sureness. The wonderful and fortunate thing about River is that she never accumulates more than she can comfortably bare. Always ready to relinquish acquisitions and release the residue from tarnished waters, River is truly free.

She has found the benefits of both worlds and, as she retains the richness of her history and her development, so does she also expand past the damns of yesterday. Story emerges new and different everyday. New opportunities with moments of insights and clarity, new horizons and landscapes all layered in colorful possibilities, make themselves known as needed.

Someday, River's story will carry her to the end of the reality that was hers. She will arrive at the ocean time of her life and she will join with the great vastness which she has heard so much about. In fact, she is certain that at times, in much stillness along the way, she has felt the presence of this great vastness stirring her waters with awe and anticipation. She holds no fear. She has been true to her intent, as her motion remains clear and powerful. Though she loved each moment in and of itself and would not choose to rush her journey, when the time comes and she arrives at Ocean, she will make this homecoming with inner calm and comfort. Then, before joining the heavenly vastness, she will settle her waters and seek a reflection. Story dances a reflection, including waves of merriment and harsh, pulling tides, as well as softly whispered memories and reminders. She has done well. Now tired and fulfilled by this review, River is ready. Quietly, gently, and with intention to do so, River lets leave of her separateness. She merges with the great vastness and is met with unconditional love and joyous welcome. She is home. Though some may have doubts about it, River's journey is not over. It has only just begun, again. Now with a new depth and a larger meaning, an expanded Story continues.

There are many events in one's lifetime, which induce the expansion of consciousness by offering waves of altered perception. For me, pregnancy and birth, motherhood and ecstatic love, and losses, including the loss of my dear father, combined with the willingness and desire to expand, were all vistas that served as reality-altering experiences. Sometimes in ecstasy and sometimes in sorrow, a fracture in reality can occur. That fracture slowly chips away at static boundaries and stretches one beyond rigid limits. Throughout the refining process of life, as we sit around the great round table and converse with societal echoes of "should's" and "should not's," it is not surprising to think that we eventually have to come face to face with the dreaded, two-headed serpent that forces each of us to face our most hidden challenges or deepest fears as we acknowledge all aspects of self. How we face that serpent will determine much about our story's unfolding path.

Table Talk

And what have you to offer to the world?

... silence

Your worth, what is your worth?

... silence

What skills do you have?

Are you a professional, a doctor or a lawyer,

or perhaps a trade?

A carpenter?

... silence

Well, how are we to place a value on you?

... a soft and understanding grin, a gentle voice.

Silence now interrupted,

and what is the sound of a feather falling through space?

... a new silence,

tables turned.

1981

$\mathcal{T}$ ABLE $\mathcal{T}$ALK, $\mathcal{T}$ABLES $\mathcal{T}$urned

Who has not had the experience of placing critical judgment on another's actions or behaviors only to later find oneself in a similar position? It takes only a heartbeat, or better yet an impulse, to turn a perfectly set table into an uproar. Then, with tables turned, those old words are very haunting and increasingly hard to swallow. The old Proverbs, "Be careful or you will eat your words… ," "What goes around comes around," or how about," Don't judge a woman until you have walked a mile in her moccasins," can suddenly strike an uncomfortably true chord. We could take a lesson here and lower the critical antenna and, in effect, give everyone a break, oneself included. That feels good and definitely creates more harmony in life. Still, there remain those unexpected moments in life where the tables do turn of their own accord, and there is spin out and discord that only yield when persistent helping voices demand that it do so.

I am remembering my time working as a hospice social worker. There were many trials and tribulations associated with that environment while heralding frequent life-and-death transitions. That time presented many challenges, making it essential to embody new abilities necessary for personal growth and transformation and for assisting families throughout their changing times. As a professional and as someone committed to being of service, I was prepared to use those tools. Recognizing the signs of impending death, it was necessary to put aside my own fears and sadness so I could be present for others as needed. It was customary for me to honor those losses with poems for those who passed. In that way I hoped they would know they were not forgotten or taken for granted. I sang to the light beyond death, and I wrote about the tenuous journey. I cried the tears and felt the pain and continued on. Life was filled with funerals and meetings, and plans for improving the quality of existence for those still living and yet waiting for their time. I witnessed and participated in decisions and choices about life-saving measures, and in painstaking discussions with philosophical questions about ethical matters.

One day I received a phone call from a minister who was near the end of her earth-time journey. She wanted help with her transition and asked me to assist. I was honored. I saw her once or twice a week for four weeks. It was indeed a rare privilege to spend time with that remarkable woman and her family. They were all so brave and so bending to the will and progression of the moment. I watched as the minister disavowed her daily responsibilities and with determination removed the threads that were woven throughout a lifetime of commitments. I sat with her and noticed how turning inward with introspection now offered her an invisible shield as she prepared for her rites of passage. That was honored by her family and friends. While sitting with her I guided her toward the light with imagery made very accessible through hypnotic channels. I held her hands and sang melodies created in the heart which beckoned to the angels in waiting. I bade her to go to the music and let it carry her gently to the love and light. She traveled and traveled, and each time she came back a little less in body. I used energy therapies to help remove blocks and opened pathways through which serenity could find her.

When she passed it was with ceremony and dignity, in the presence of her loved ones who were willing to let her go. I found this experience both enriching and melancholy, witnessing what we humans experience as a separation from loved ones in a clearer and deeper manner. I lingered over thoughts of life, death and eternity, and wondered over the paradox of coping with loss and pain while going through this separation, even with full knowledge of the beauty and glory found in the beyond. I thought about the purpose of all this life-and-death changing of realities, and pondered my specific purpose.

In the evenings at home with my children of about two and four years of age, I felt the power of motherhood surge through my blood and the ancient possessive tug for survival. I knew in that moment the need to protect them and to love them, to keep them warm and safe, and to secure them in their pristine version of reality. What mother does not vow to keep the clouds from encroaching on a worry-free childhood? This all occurred in May 1991.

Crossing Over

Where are you now?
In clouded images...?
Submerged in comprehension
while fragmented circular words appear and sound on lips?
Where only whispers dare to free themselves
gently from the great abyss?

The murmurs are familiar and yet out of reach,
of no concern now...
I see you through a long and narrowing tunnel.
As I expand,
perspective and relativity vanish...

Can you understand me?
I reach through the abyss and call to you...

You lower your face so full of love and life,
then sweetly put your ear against my mouth...

Frustration lingers,
dizzy with anxiety over the crumbling bridge.
Hot blood pounding, she is leaving, she is leaving...

Forgive me as I go...
I must cross over,
for now, the bridge is down.

1991

It was October of the same year that tables turned for me. It was autumn, with fully turning colors, changing and arousing new awareness about life going to rest and waiting for the spring renewal. A time where it cannot be ignored that all things come and pass. Every day an illustrious demonstration that none are spared nor are they denied this passage of time. It was a true autumn. The earth was blanketed with piles of dying reminders as the trees stoically stood their ground, patiently waiting for their new splendor. It was in this autumn that I would be challenged to expand and integrate my trust that yes, splendor and new life would return.

A True Autumn

So light upon the gentle breeze
bronzed and gold as falling leaves.
Dancing with the eagle now
with grace and sweet serenity,
enchanted with eternity.

A true autumn of life appears
the willow sheds with mournful tears.
Yearning to hold tight once more
so embraced, so adored.
A silhouette, a thread too sheer
reflects a life that can't be here.
A shimmer or a fading light
beckons to the darkened night.

A true autumn of life appears
the distant horizon surrenders and clears.
The willow bends and ends her grief
releasing love, then finds relief.
Dancing with the eagle now
with grace and sweet serenity,
replenished through eternity.
A lightened heart, a peaceful soul
dancing now as autumn takes toll.

to dad with love

1991

$\mathcal{A}$ True Autumn

As a child I found my father to be a composite of everything soft and warm and precious to a little girl's heart. I lived for the moment that he would show himself home from work, and then held him as my captive audience and companion. Cocooned in his unconditional love and understanding and shielded from outside interference's, I was allowed to know myself. In turn, this self inside the young child's body served to brighten up my father's sometimes darkened world. We understood each other, and as days and months changed into passing years, our friendship deepened into an unspoken commitment to honor and protect all that was held sacred to each other.

As a boy my father was a storm waiting to break, but he seldom felt the after-calm. Feeling misunderstood and very self-conscious, he carried the torrent with him. Through adolescence, through the Marine Corps at seventeen years old which torpedoed him into adulthood, into love and marriage and fatherhood, hung a cloud of conflict around a self that was not free. I did not know that at the time, nor did I see the man who was so pained and hurt by what he saw and experienced in the world. I only saw my father--the dad who was always there for me, who heard my words and dried my tears. He was the man who was the only grown-up on the block who had all the kids call him by his first name, and they stopped to visit him as often as they could. This man brought home lonely souls to have dinner with our family, and anonymously left gifts for those less fortunate whom he befriended in the factories who were working for minimum wages and treated poorly. My father was a truck driver, and for a long time I think he enjoyed his time of being king of the road. That road, however, took him many places, including eventually to despair.

My growing-up time was a solid and stable time. I had one sister, one mom, and one dad. We lived together in the same home for all of my childhood years. I marvel now at my dad's ability to subdue his storm and raise a family with honesty, love, good humor, and responsibility. I seldom experienced any wrath or anger from him, and on the occasions when in his fatherly role it was necessary for him to discipline me, it was always very short lived. We seemed to bring out the best in each other, as two beings who were determined to nourish and be nourished by the other. I learned many things from my father as we shared a very open communication that was free of aggression or dominance and that formed my early ideal for the type of communication that was possible to exchange in the world with true and valued friends. I learned to be in good relationships with men, which served me greatly in years to come as I sought out and often found other wonderful men to have in my life. Never would I settle for being treated poorly (at least not for long) or with disrespect, nor would that be what I offered.

So I walked my years through early childhood, into adolescence, and later as an adult with a constant connection to this father who was sometimes nearby and sometimes not but always strongly with me. Along with his consistent love and committed loyalty, he had an even deeper understanding of when to freely release me to my life out in the world. Whether off to college, on a traveling adventure or finally moving to Oregon, though tears were shed, the path remained open and clear. He would never ask me to stay or to pass up an opportunity. We sent letters with poems and our latest insights, and cassettes with our thoughts and songs. Many years later my children would wonder at how I always knew when Grandpa would call. I always knew, for he was my 5 p.m. phone call. They would laugh and laugh at this magic.

When I moved to Oregon Dad would come for extended visits. Sometimes he would stay for two weeks and other times for two months. Oh, how he loved the beautiful wooded and secluded spots that Tim and I would choose for our homes. When Dad visited we had a break because he would joyfully assume all of the outdoor requirements, like feeding the chickens, feeding and playing with the goats, cutting wood, hauling water, and taking long walks and rests with the dogs. It didn't matter what, he did them and then looked for more. In fact, if a winter storm hit and we lost all power for a week, to him that was all the better. Then he'd be up at the crack of dawn, gathering snow to melt on the woodstove, making sure there was plenty of flushing water. He simply relished and thrived on mastering a natural life in the woods. Evenings were his favorite as he lit candles and breathed in the peace and serenity of this quiet world. He needed the quiet now more than ever. His storm was brewing a strong discontentment with life, as the sometimes harsh and bitter reality that can be found on Earth was engulfing his perspective. He was becoming a seemingly hard and desperate man who tragically loved beauty more than anyone I had ever known and yet was losing his ability to find it or create it in his life. His spirit, the very soul that knew so well how to let me soar, was dying, and I began to grieve, already anticipating that great loss. I found it unbearable to watch him decline, as he did over a period of ten years or more. In this decade of life, Tim and Dad also grew very close. Tim quickly transformed from Dad's great joking comment of "Who are you dragging off the plane now?" when I first brought Tim home to Michigan to meet the family, into the dear and devoted son that he never had. Tim was equal to me in his eagerness to call and share with Dad all the momentous events in our lives. Dad, in turn, vicariously joined in the highs and lows of those occasions, shepherding us when he felt it necessary, under his vast and protective wings, and rejoicing triumphantly at our victories. Through uprooting moves, financial depressions, and multiple miscarriages, Dad remained a steadfast anchor determined to keep us afloat and out of the storm even as he was losing ground with his own.

Throughout those years he found that a routine of extreme exercise, caring for his fish and plants, and reading would help to pass his time more comfortably. He walked many miles daily and rode his bike with a fury that set his mind free and clear, just as highs and lows of understanding and wisdom flooded him with a turbulence that also ignited his longing. We interpreted that longing in many ways, but I can see clearly now that it was his true longing to be touched once again by a spirit who could shine down light and illuminate beauty and reason in his life, and most importantly illuminate the reason *for* his life. Having felt misunderstood for so long he needed to be recognized for who he was, a man waiting to be calmed and stilled, a man longing to be the *gentle* that he felt in his heart but could not always show, a man craving to live in peace, and a man wanting beauty bestowed on the earthly existence that was once known and still remembered by his soul.

I knew this to be true, because it was also what I wanted and it was what we unspokenly understood in each other. He always said that he had the strong body and I had the strong will and spirit. That may be so, since what he was so unable to do for himself was what he did so well for me. He created beauty and joy for me, in the form of absolute acceptance of me, and that gave me the freedom to believe in and trust in myself. His generosity allowed me to move easily in life. I could enmesh myself in light and love to use as a shield in life, whereas he had no shield to serve him. Life became very heavy for him. In paradox to his longing for a peaceful retreat, his perspective of a bitter and dark reality encroached upon him more and narrowed his options for escape. My father hardened. Conversations were frequently more in appeasement now. I frantically wanted to return to him the unlimited love and acceptance which he had so freely always given to me. I fiercely honored and respected his wisdom, protected his sensitivities, and nourished his right to express himself as needed. I paved the way for his comfort and smooth sailing, and kept a constant look-out for obstacles in his path's way. Still, even as I made sure that the coast was clear for his easy maneuvering, I myself became a challenge to him. The deeper he went into bleak and fatalistic thinking, the stronger I grieved as a void was forming in my heart. I countered his words with suggestions and ideas for regaining beauty and meaning in his life. He mused over suicide as I spoke of life and love, of grandchildren and of healing. He held the concept of suicide as a carrot dangling off in the distance but still in reach to be grabbed if desperately needed. I held in my heart the power of healing. I could truly envision this happening for him, as I never lost sight of his higher self. He had so many gifts, including his complete respect for the natural world.

Watching my dad plant a tree reflected the same feeling, as would an artist driven by perfection. Free of time constraints or any reason to hurry, Dad moved in a gentle and quiet manner on the land. Preparing the soil and preparing the tree was done with intuitive ceremony. I am certain that at those times he experienced the peace and harmony that comes only from truly feeling the oneness of all things and one's place in that oneness. He also possessed a tender love and understanding for all children. Through all his ups and downs he maintained a loving relationship with all four of his grandchildren. His sense of humor and quaking laughter were glorious to witness. It seemed at those times he could take flight from his earthbound condition and freely delight, for the moment, in the pleasure of humor.

As time passed there were daily phone conversations, weekly visits, hopes and disappointments, and a lingering flirtation with loss. On countless occasions Tim would come home and know immediately that I had been speaking to Dad. Though largely left unspoken, Tim and I both knew that in some insidious way I was beginning to fade with Dad. It would have been almost sacrilegious to speak of that. I had too much love for Dad, and Tim had too much love and respect for both of us. We lived with that daily paradox. Tim and I together with the kids had a wonderful life rich in love and creativity. We were surrounded by nature in our country home and thrived in that existence together. Yet, the undercurrent could not be ignored, and finally came the crash. Dad had a major heart attack in June 1991. Out for a bike ride and after extreme pain in his chest, he walked his bike home, carried it down the basement, and sat in the kitchen for hours. Then, judging it time to go to the hospital, he notified my mom. Tanned as the autumn leaves and toned as a much younger man, after just going through a crushing blow to his heart, he entered the hospital barely paled by the experience. When Tim and I arrived a couple of hours later he was sitting up and drinking chicken soup. He was looking calm but obviously worried for me, it is now a surreal image to remember. Though hidden from view, the damage to his heart had been done. A large area of frontal heart muscle had been damaged and we were told it would remain so and worsen.

For his recuperating stay in the hospital, my father was described by the nurses as "pacing like a caged animal" and so he was. He wrestled with panic, anxiety, and self-renunciation. He faced the realization that his failure to seek out immediate medical attention now left him with a condition that would ultimately lead to the demise of his physical strength which he so valued, and it was irreversible. That loss represented so much, both in the pride that he took from remaining strong and fit but most importantly the loss of the very physical activities which had been his lifeline for survival and coping. So he paced like an animal out of sorts with his life and troubled by his environment until he was released and set free to go home. There, his depression deepened. His days turned into what he called nightmares, as his perspective inverted and strangled any possible fragments of hope, and his void filled with more serious contemplations of suicide. There were trials with Prozac which terrorized him as his anxiety grew with the taking. We had countless phone conversations and shared many visits. I pleaded for him to accept my encouragement, to seek outside help, and to see the vision that I stubbornly maintained for him. I insisted on holding on. He waited for me to let go. It was my nature to see and trust in so many possibilities. Still, even as I continually rebutted with alternatives, my heart understood his need and his right to end his suffering. Over the years I had supported clients who were suffering from what were considered to be terminal illnesses as they chose to decline further treatment. They were intelligent, reasonable, and wonderful human beings who had the right to make that choice. I knew that this was true for my father as well.

By now it was late summer and everyone was over to celebrate my thirty-eighth birthday. As always, Dad and I managed to go off and find a place for private discussions. We were sitting at a picnic table, across from each other, and having one of our *distant* but heavy talks about suicide options. It was distant because it still felt impossible and unreal, and not like something that could really happen. Denial's mask was more pervasive and had a stronger hold than I ever would have imagined. I felt so open and capable of handling those questions of life and death. At least, I was with my clients. There was a terrible split occurring within me. Again, even in my most heated challenges to Dad's perspective, I knew that I had to honor him. I had to let him go but didn't know how I could. One night I had a dream where he was walking with a cane and looking very old and tired. In the dream he fell and I suddenly realized that it was over. I seemed to understand that letting him go was the highest love I could offer.

In that way my birthday came and went. The weeks did not stand still. Telephone conversations became more peaceful even as he retained his hold on the elusive act of suicide. I instead allowed that concept to diffuse into some unreal event of the future. I suppose that was the only way that I could cope. After all, his "just in case" death wish had been around for so long, surely it would remain unfulfilled.

It was early fall. Squirrels gathered their acorns and replenished their hoards as the geese journeyed to warmer lands, and the turtles and frogs made their beds for a long winter dream. All prepared, as they must for the approaching season of darkened days. Many humans fretfully watch as the daylight shortens and many have hearts that sink with that anticipation. My heart does not sink. I am fortunate to be one who loves all of the seasons. My light is not dimmed by a cloudy day. I hope that will also be true for my children, and that they can find beauty in all days. I cannot bear to think that their tender hearts would sadden on a cloud-filled day.

It was the weekend, October 5th. Dad called many times. He asked me if Tim knew that he loved him as a son, not a son-in-law. Innocently, I assured him that this was known by Tim. Sunday was welcomed by another call. That time I was told how much I meant to him and what our special relationship had done for him over the years. I was deeply moved and echoed the same back to him. It was not a tense call. It was a call about love. Monday, October 7th found Tim at work while the children and I were at play. Another phone call. It was not Dad. It was a police officer calling from Mom and Dad's house. His words were clear and to the point: Dad was dead and Mom was alone; could I get there as soon as possible to be with her? Mom got on the phone and we shared in the numbness that traveled through the telephone line. He really did it. My dad, who couldn't leave his circumstances and travel to a distant island (he was there during the war and longed to return) as he so often spoke of, my dad who couldn't make his dreams come true, my dad who hated the violence in the world, had done it. My dad pulled the trigger--and I fell to the floor. When I got up I reached for the phone and called Tim. I blurted out what had happened. He cried all the way home. I prepared for handling the children, who were two-and-a-half and four years old. When Tim arrived home we told them that Grandpa had died of a heart attack. We said that his heart had stopped working. I guess that in some ways that was true. Our little boy cried as he tried to understand the meaning of this event. He went around saying that "Grandpa's heart was broken," and then he wondered when it would get fixed. He wondered for a long time, and so did I. Our daughter, who even at the young age of four was sometimes fearful of intense emotion, allowed her heart to spill over and sobbed in our arms as each of us in our own way shared in the deep sorrow over the loss of Grandpa.

I made arrangements for the kids to spend the night with friends. We felt they needed some shielding from the intense chaos and pain that we would soon be immersed in at Grandma's. So we dropped them off and started out to Mom's. I do not remember the drive. With the children safe and snug and

Tim behind the wheel, I was free to dissolve. I dove into a great convoluting sea of quicksand and just kept going deeper.

A Soul's Infinite Echo

A cry of pain crashes like the waves against rocks
deeper than the depths of the sea itself.
Shouting out towards space,
bouncing in a frenzy of unknown obstacles and unforeseen ironies.
A soul's infinite echo resounds a fury.

Fighting to break free, to win the tug of war.
All the tugs of war.
Waves crashing thunderous echoes resounding on unmapped territory.
Undirected, unleashed, raw power.
The power and pain of transcending.
Seeking clarity and balance, a soul's infinite echo resounds a fury.

Desperately demanding resolution.

Thrashing aimlessly about in chaotic motion.

Spinning, whirling...

Energy once abundant, now slowing, dulling into reverie.

Slowed motion blurs a tumultuous vision.

A soul's infinite echo resounds, then yields to inner direction.

1985

The Infinite Journey

Arriving at Moms was a horror. I slinked out of the car and up the porch steps. Clinging to the side of the house and slowing my feet, I did not want to enter. Entering the house where Dad no longer was became an emptiness and a truth I did not want to face. Yet, however slow my footsteps, and however much I stalled, I still found myself in the house hugging my mom amidst a clamor of quiet unrest. With voices respectfully softened and activities stilled, there was already a murmur of plans and tasks to attend to. In that way, pain is pushed to where it cannot interfere, the body moves as though owned by another, and life begins again. There are funeral arrangements to be made, memorial services to be planned, meals, phone calls, friends, the children, and the whole array of social and cultural agendas literally demanding attention. Weak-kneed suffering or even soul searching are afforded precious little time. The dead are tended to by social protocols, economics, and politics, while the living are buried by the weight and restrictions of those codes. Finally there was a *visit* with Dad, a viewing of his body in the casket. He looked so pale and I longed for his sun-bronzed skin. With his arms folded across his chest, he was the uncanny quiet that death brings which was so contrary to his commonly tense and agitated manner. That was gone, but seeing my dad in the casket evoked that involuntary reflex of choking convulsions that ripple through the body during times of enormous strain and breathlessness. I could not move or breathe until finally, relieved by torrents of sobs which allowed me to collapse by his side, I surrendered to their releasing force. Dad's storm was over and mine was just beginning. As I left his side, I was then ushered to the office where final arrangements were made. Composure was regained as lifelessness was born within me.

Back at Mom's, it was soon time to pick up the children from our friends and then wait to face tomorrow's funeral. It all just kept moving. Some airing of words needed to be spoken between some family members. Mother, sister, uncle and myself clearing some resentment over past deeds, while our family of varying needs and emotions settled into a deeper level of biological connection and understanding. We were family quietly together; few harsh words were exchanged. We simply did what we had to do, each of us with the generous intention of trying not to disturb the other. Do not disturb or ruffle, or cause any more pain. Pain became the common denominator which was greatly respected by all.

In life, some of us cry and some of us cannot. Each of us in our own way grappled with what felt like a tragic and perhaps needless loss. The very nature of the individuality and style of grief can promote the feeling of separateness, thus in itself reinforcing an ensuing isolation. As we retreated inwards there was a narrowing of what could be shared about that condition. Yet even within that personal insulation there was the common ability for all of us to share our memories of Dad. Much can be said about Dad's style and sense of humor. In fact, he left with a flare of humor that still puts a smile on my face. Though his lean and athletic body did not boast of it, Dad loved to eat and thoroughly disliked being restricted in his choices. With his genetically high cholesterol Mom attempted to offer her "guidance," especially in regards to eating the forbidden egg. Dad loved eggs. When living with Tim and me in Oregon, Dad relished the country-fresh eggs which our dear chickens generously provided. Back at home he dreaded the deprivation of the removal of the yoke, or worse, the no-egg diet. Before *leaving* he decided to make his final statement on that subject. He did that by leaving a plate of egg whites, with the yokes missing, resting in the sink just waiting to be found. Dad enjoyed a yoke feast for his last meal. That may sound morbid to some, but it was not unlike the other jokes or tricks he left around the house from time to time. For me it reflected that though he had lost a lot in life, he had not lost his intrinsic sense of humor. That remains important to me, because it is a lasting remnant of the light I saw deep within him even when he could not. Through our tears of remembering and our tears of missing him, we all acknowledged that Dad had the last word on the subject of eggs.

It is a yo-yo-like routine that can keep us first, retracting back to the haven of self and next, reaching out to others to share a common moment, that quickly becomes the normal routine in life while grieving. Life has a new flow, and for each coming day, for many days and many months to come, there will be a continuing of that juggling of the self which can be extended to others and that which must be kept for safe keeping.

The funeral came and went in a fog. There was a little gathering, a little poetry read of both Dad's and mine, but little satisfaction for me. Dad was taken to a stark cemetery where the earth's abundance was not felt. There was no beauty around and once again Dad had to *fit* where he could not. That would not be where I would visit him. I would honor him at a place that he loved and where he created beauty-- at our home that we called Turtle Creek Farm, on the land which we all cared for. We used to call Dad our landscaper. He loved to mow the land and make certain areas look like a park. When Dad stayed with us it wasn't long before we heard the humming of the riding tractor. What a familiar picture comes to mind: Dad with his red bandana in place on his head while wearing his blue denim cut-off shorts (short shorts because he loved to show off his tanned and fit legs) and boots. He'd ride the mower the way he drove, slow and patiently, and for that period he would ride his blues into oblivion. He planted many trees, often blue spruces, which became lovely celebrations on the land. Three of those trees formed a circle with a nice grassy center. Years earlier when Brutus, Mom and Dad's beloved Norwegian Elkhound, died, we buried his collar in the middle of that tree circle as we said our good-byes to him. Dad loved Brutus dearly and he loved those trees, so that would be the perfect spot. That would be where I would visit Dad; certainly, much of his energy was already there. Later we came to hold a memorial there with other friends who loved Dad and either could not make it to the funeral or, like myself, were simply not satisfied there. We set a date, notified friends and, very importantly, we prepared the land. The lawn was long into field now and wet, so we painstakingly mowed a large circle around the trees and planted mums in the center. It was beautiful. I was ready to say a more proper good-bye to Dad and help all hearts to be more at rest.

I grew more and more agitated as each day grew nearer to the Memorial Day. Once again there would be poetry to share, mostly Dad's. I wanted others to share in that part of him, but I began to wonder if I could hold up to it all with so many people and so much conversation. I felt at a loss. For most of my life I had been the counselor, social worker, hypnotherapist, teacher, etc. In those roles there had been little room for sharing my vulnerabilities and usually little desire to do so. I had been held in high regard for my abilities and my strengths. That shaped an image which somehow had to be upheld. Now, that had to be forgotten. I was raw and felt bare to the bone. No attempts would be made to hide that. It was time to walk feeling vulnerable and exposed which, unknown to me at the time, would prove to be a groundbreaking experience, paving the road for future healing and growing.

Friends came and we gathered together to hold a circle for Dad. We held his place in our memories and in my mind I claimed a spot for him. There was a great stillness and a touching of hearts, with the sharing of stories and later the sharing of food as well. Even the children held their place and their presence in the circle. I was so proud of them and felt ever more strongly both their loss and Dad's. They would no longer be bathed in his adoring and unfaltering love, and he would not share in the tender and precious moments throughout their growing-up years which he had so loved to bear witness to.

Finally the day was over, the children in bed, and Tim and I, exhausted from the day's events, cleaned up and went to bed. In the darkness, held close in Tim's arms, I simply curled up tighter and smaller, as small as I could, surprised to find that I was still there. I was visible and my life was still present and known. Graced with sleep I faded into dreamtime, praying for a visit with Dad.

With each day came a deeper and more painful recognition that Dad was gone. Everything else seemed to be the same. I had the same responsibilities in life, such as family, work, and preparing for art shows that we were soon to participate in. I continued beading, caring for the children, and seeing clients. At a glance no one would ever know that our family had just gone through an incredible trauma. In my heart it was incongruous to imagine that I was even standing and functioning at all. I felt torn and somewhat guilty because I had not collapsed. My world felt very surreal. I knew that in many ways all eyes were upon me. My relationship with Dad had been very profound, with our love so deep and our lives so linked. Everyone was wondering how I would survive his loss. He, who had been my loving anchor and support in life, my super fan and protector from all "evils," was gone. I was still present and much seemed the same, but in my grief I had lost sight of the light. Reclaiming the light in my life would prove to be a worthy journey.

Now Gone

A shiver down my spine
now tells me you're gone.
A new existence
too fast to comprehend ...
one blink.
Here, now gone. Yet nothing changes.
All remains as it was.
The view out my window
is no different.
Snowflakes fall and melt into earth.
They too have lived their lives.
And I will not see you again.

1987

$\mathcal{N}$ OW GONE

It is true that new realities and self concepts emerge as old ones are literally blown away. One bullet takes one life and scatters many others somewhere into the abyss. There are many chasms wherein lie treasures of light, including wit and humor, love and beauty, courage and strength, all of which are the light and shining attributes of life. When separated from their host they wait to be reunited with those to whom they have been lost. I found myself waiting, too, for their return.

My sister and I were having a phone conversation one day as we were checking in on one another. It was one of many conversations to come where we would go from mundane warm-up checks to the deep and heavy in the next breath. We were on new territory and it would take a while to figure out how to talk together without nervous hesitation. There was an unspoken seeking or desire to rediscover normalcy in our relationship. For a time all felt very strange and strained. We fell upon the subject of Dad and suicide and how all this was perceived by *others*. It was suddenly very shocking to realize how we were perceived by others. Dad was gone and we, along with Mom, were the survivors. That was generally the common lingo. We were now the family members who were considered "at risk." It was not another family being discussed at work or in a professional meeting. *We* were being watched, and even watching one another, for signs of distress. That was a startling revelation, a flash of insight, a glimpse into the impenetrable. There was a silence on the phone as each of us unwittingly visited with that new piece of self. I would continue to wrestle with that for a while.

I had not quite figured out the whole suicide thing. In fact, for a long time I did not call it a suicide. People who are considered terminally ill sometimes end their lives to end their suffering. Some refuse treatment, others refuse sustenance, while others overdose on their meds. Is that suicide or a merciful death? Dad had been depressed for a long time and kept the concept of suicide as a "safety valve" or an emergency exit. That's all, just a concept that he never even attempted. Then he had a major heart attack and lost what had previously sustained him, his health and his pride. He became ill with a failing heart which would not improve. Doctors could not tell him at what rate the degeneration would continue to occur. He was fearful of another heart attack with heroic actions taken. He did not want heroic measures and was uncertain that his will would be respected. At that point the concept of suicide became tangible to his senses and he began making plans. We even discussed them but I didn't believe in them. I didn't recognize that he had made a shift. He had reached the point where he was prepared to end his suffering and he did. He put a bullet in his heart and died alone. Was that any different from others who refused treatment or sought an assisted suicide? Dad was clear in what he was doing; he knew what he wanted. I was not clear and was ever confused about what it all meant and what I would do with it. Through soul searching in the months and years to come I would continue to ponder that dilemma.

It was 10 months later when my very dear dog friend, Arnuk, had a stroke. Arnuk, an outstanding Norwegian Elkhound, had been my loyal companion through thick and thin for the last 14 and a half years. On August 1st, 1992 it happened. I was with him when, after finishing his meal, he simply fell down. He lost all control of his bodily functions and could not stand up. I was horrified as I watched him desperately drag his back legs in trying to move forward. He wanted to go outside, so Tim and I assisted him. I wanted to go into denial and pretend that he would get better, but I knew that he would not. I sat with him and watched him suffer. Grief stricken, I knew that it was time to call the vet and ask him to come out. I had so hoped that when his time came, Arnuk would die a natural death. As I sat with him while waiting for the vet, I went back and forth over my feelings about humans interfering with the dying process of their animal loved ones and wished that Arnuk could just wait for his death. However, I loved him so much, and when I looked at him I knew I had to let him go. I had to arrange to help him pass. I was with Arnuk when he received his lethal injection. It took only a moment and he was peacefully gone.

I did not feel the same relief. I felt like I had been thrown against a wall, again. I sobbed for Arnuk, for Dad, and for all the world's losses as a great, infinite pit opened inside me. Finally tired and weakened, I realized so clearly, so easily what should have been obvious but had evaded me. I simply wasn't prepared for those deaths. Intellectually, philosophically, and even spiritually, I accepted death and one's right to choose death, but I wasn't prepared for the great ramifications. I was swimming with thoughts, wondering why I had to agree to let go of another loved one. At least Arnuk died with love and companionship, but not Dad. He died alone and with a bullet through his heart. That would be my next battle. Acknowledging the violence of this act was an agony for me. Why did it have to be a bullet? I tried to imagine what it would be like to actually come to the place where he could really pull the trigger. Could he have been that sure and that ready to leave? No mistakes would happen. If one puts a bullet through the heart, that will successfully end a life. Was he really that desperate to end his nightmare? I could not fathom being at that place in life. Dad often said he was a loner and thus did he die. I could not hold his hand, or sing him to the light, and painfully, we did not say good-bye.

Regardless of my inner turmoil, after Dad died I steadfastly stood by his decision. I missed him terribly and at the same time defended his right of choice. Close friends questioned me and waited for my anger to emerge. It did not. Some shared with me their anger and indignation. They wondered how he could do this to me and the whole family. I would not indulge in that thinking and remained fierce in my loyalty to Dad. After all, was he not the same person who gently nurtured me along as a child while protecting my fragile core? Didn't he always offer me unconditional love and respect? It was my turn to maintain the same for him. I felt that even the slightest deviation from that would be a betrayal, and in my heart of hearts I truly understood his decision. I knew him so well, and long suffered over his circumstances. With my conscious refusal to look beyond my total commitment of loyalty and acceptance, my dreamtime mind took over and mastered a different plan, a plan that involved insights and revelations which ultimately would lead to the next step in my healing transformation.

They began with what I called my *visits* with Dad, where we would be involved in various different scenarios. I enjoyed those visits because they helped to satisfy my need to see him. That was one of my deep longings. I wanted Dad to appear to me. There were plenty of reports of those kinds of appearances where loved ones had received apparitions. Why wasn't Dad visiting me in that way? Soon the dreams took on a new shape and purpose. Denial began to emerge. In those new manifestations Dad would come to me in dreamtime and tell me that it was all a mistake and that he wasn't really dead. Of course, that was the dream I had been waiting for. Who doesn't want to be told that their nightmare was only a dream?

At first the dreams were very plain as they spoke of that misunderstanding. Later they became elaborate schemes trying to convince me of that truth so that I could be the messenger. I was supposed to report Dad's return. I would awaken from those denials only to re-experience the reality of my waking state, and rediscover the other truth about Dad. That soon became very draining, leaving me feeling very strange and sad. On the one hand, I loved seeing him in dreams so we could spend time together. Yet, what was the attempt at illusion about? Was I growing too tired and confused? Then it hit me. The dreams measured and reflected the level of my increasing desperation. The more desperate I became about his loss, the more elaborate the attempt would be to convince me that it wasn't so. I shared my insight with Tim, and I knew those dreams had to stop. They were interfering with my life, and left me feeling dull and in the middle of two conflicting realities.

It was growing increasingly difficult to communicate and relate to others. I could go to work and see clients and that would work out fine. With clients I automatically made the shift to their world and so I was present with them. The session was for them and their lives, so I could easily enter my usual role as the facilitator for their desired transformation. That was often a comfort for me. While facilitating their journeys, my reality also had to shift, such that I was able to function at a much higher level. The rest of the time I lived in a fog. Even playing with the kids was like reaching out through a very long tunnel. Everything and everyone was very distant. It was just two months since Dad had left, and presumably life was back to "normal." Superficially that was true.

Tim and I were getting ready to participate in the upcoming winter art shows. Normally I loved those shows. Regardless of what was sold, there were always friends and acquaintances galore, other artists to trade with, networking and updating about resources, and a fun time for Tim and me to share together. That had all changed. Throughout the show I was only there in body. My spirit and heart were off nursing the wounds that were left by the splintering trauma that had occurred in my life. In the evening, after a long and awful day, suffering through trying to keep up smiles and pretences, we went home and I finally let down. Going to bed exhausted, I had another dream visit. That time I took control. Dad and I were seated across from one another, as we had been on so many past occasions, fully engrossed in conversation. Again, Dad was telling me about the mistake, that he had not really died. I stopped him from continuing on with that desperate escapade. I explained that though I loved visiting with him and wanted more visits with him, they had to be honest. I delineated that it was just too draining to remain on the roller coaster of conflicting realities. I confessed that I knew he was dead and that was that. When I awoke I immediately remembered my dream and, though saddened by the stark realization, I think I felt a little triumphant as well. There would be no more denial--other issues and pain to work through, but not denial. Dad was gone from my current reality and I knew that it was so.

Dad, Tim, and I used to love to talk about the phenomenon of time and all its possibilities. One favorite topic of ours was time travel. We looked at all aspects from heart to science that could or would explain why time travel was or wasn't possible. Dad had a thirst for those conversations, and Tim and I were the perfect candidates with whom to share and test his theories. The elusive concept of time that we humans hold so dear is something I still love to ponder over. It is said that time heals all. Over the next months and years to come I would have the opportunity to more fully comprehend the benefit of time well used and its ability to elicit a healing alchemy.

Time And The Fool

Time.

Tic-toc.

Tic-toc.

Trick.

A trickster of Puc's own delight.
And who has forgotten to reset the clock?

The fool looks towards eternity
and laughs.

1981

$\mathcal{T}$IME AND HEALING Alchemy

Eternity was another of Dad's favorite words and subjects to study and scrutinize. He spent a good deal of his waking hours pleasuring and agonizing over the ideas of an infinite and eternal universe. He just couldn't get enough of it, nor could he quiet his mind from that thinking. He would shape and re-shape his hypothesis about this infinite foreverness, about evolution, or why the Big Bang Theory did not hold up to his analysis. It wasn't at all unusual for Dad to call up just to share his latest thoughts. I often thought of him traveling with sages and having firsthand other-dimensional experiences. Back on Earth, I was still waiting for him to come calling as one earth-year had already gone by since his passing.

It was time to go back to the gravesite for the Jewish tradition of unveiling the gravestone. My agitation again increased, as the day grew nearer. I dreaded going back to his grave once again to participate in something which felt foreign and empty to me, especially since I knew it held no meaning for Dad. So with the desire to honor Dad and to put meaning in a ceremony for him (and for me), I wrote and read a short memorial. My life had always been in pursuit of meaning, and what I found long ago was that if it could not be found then it had to be created. That was also true for beauty and all other attributes of light and love. In the midst of creating the memorial, my heart was stirred, breathing became shallow, and the agitation stubbornly persisted. Another great quake, one of which I remained consciously unaware, was simmering within and soon would boil over into dreamtime.

One year since Dad's death, and healing felt evasive and absent. Instead, 365 days of time had gone by, with each day pounding the reality of my loss deeper and deeper into my psyche. Each and every cell in my body reverberated with that news. My communication was still poor and in some ways I lost confidence. That was new and uncomfortable for me. Signs of rage would show themselves with a lack of patience and easy irritation. I would apologize to the children for those moments of shortcomings. I would briefly explain that I missed Grandpa and was having a difficult time. With heavy hearts and saddened faces, and somewhat shy about the great wounding that had affected us, they seemed to understand. Very young children are often amateurs when it comes to intense emotional pain which threatens to rock their naturally more self-oriented world. However, my little Jacy confronted his pain and confusion by play-acting about hearts not working in his favorite stuffed animals, and by asking countless questions about Grandpa. At two and-a-half years old he was already quite an expert at dealing with his feelings. On the other hand, my dear Shandra was most comfortable when the subject was left unbroached. She was very uneasy and uncertain about her brother's audacity to speak of Grandpa's death and was concerned that it would be disturbing for me. I worried about that for Shandra and was grateful for Jacy's ease and perseverance. Eventually Shandra would also relax with the matter. In fact, with the discussions that Jacy's questions and play behavior would evoke, I think she came to realize that pain was tangible and could be spoken about, and that our emotional selves would still be safe. I was glad that we addressed these things because I did not want Shandra to be lonely with her feelings. I also emphatically wanted the children to remember their Grandpa. I wanted them to have the joy of humorous memories and to know that just like expressing pain and sadness, laughter was also safe to permit. So, as time went on, we shared in many cherished moments, laughing in loving memory as we recounted stories about Grandpa's many charms. We remembered how he would surprise us in the morning by coming over for an unannounced visit. The children would delight in seeing the white bakery bag in his hand filled with muffins and chocolate chip cookies, which quickly became his trademark! It was also a family joke about how Grandma would love to go shopping for the grandchildren and Grandpa, who hated to shop, would then find the set aside stash of gifts and steal them off to the grandkids while Grandma was at work. He just couldn't wait to see their expressions of exuberance, and Grandma did not mind his indulgence. Many of those shared memories took place in the car as we scurried to and fro in our world. It was then that I became famous for always missing my turn. Engrossed in our memories I would drive right by our destination and as I turned around there were great groans to be heard in the backseat.

During that period of my life dreams continued to play the role of therapy and therapist. They were able to probe and dig through to the depths of my well guarded fortress. No stone was left unturned in their honorable attempt to find insights and resolutions, and that endeavor was not left unrewarded. Finally, there was a breakthrough that would force me to face the forbidden truth.

Anger arose and I could not escape its direct challenge. It was time for a confrontation. The dream was a long intertwining collage depicting messages which included my need to stand on my own two feet, my attempts at denial, and feelings of abandonment and disappointment. At the end of the dream it surged into a volcanic eruption of anger as I repeated over and over again, "yes, I am angry, I am angry." Crying hysterically as I repeated that to Dad, who in the dream was in his pick-up truck preparing rather stoically to leave, I begged him to come out and talk to me. He did, and then I awoke from the dream.

The fortress had crumbled. I remained in bed feeling bare and anguished over the betrayal. How could I be angry? Clearly I couldn't deny my dream, which came from that hidden reservoir where only truth was found. I swore to myself that I would not tell anyone of my discovery. It seemed divulging that information would soil my vow to support Dad's decision beyond exception, which I then felt I had failed. However, my anger chose not to live with that folly and would not settle for being ignored. Stunned, I got out of bed and slowly walked into the kitchen where Tim was already eating breakfast. I broke my oath of silence and immediately told him of my dream. Again, I insisted that I would never breathe a word of that to any other person. Not under any circumstance would I allow for Dad to be slandered. I was in a healing crisis. My "soul" plan had a life of its own. Internal movement for transformation was occurring whether I liked it or not. It could not be stopped anymore than a rampaging flood could halt its course. I resented that will for transformation, though it was my own, but eventually I would come around to accepting its necessity.

In the meantime I steadied myself in the daily activities of caregiving and nurturing my family, my clients, and my garden. The moment the children were down for a nap I plunged into the garden, where I lost myself in weeding or planting and relished being in the dirt that was up to my elbows and smeared across my face in sweat. I employed the sun and earth to lift my darkened world. I sought vision from the red-tailed hawk that soared above, and found comfort in the beauty of the flowers that displayed all the colors of the rainbow. Above all were the leafing out trees with their new green vitality that gently breathed to me in whispers that it was time to surrender. All secrets must be set free to fly.

Tree Lace Buddha

My friend, your tree spirit calls to me
and I go to meditate, while the sun,
over my shoulder,
in the west,
illuminates briefly your elegant winter skeleton.

And you have been a true friend
to hear my confessions and see my foolish ways.
In melancholy and in joy,
stories of misguided angry words,
of jealousy and painted faces.

I close my eyes and I am a child
with you my warm and stable womb.
Water suctioned through roots
flood and pulsate through you,

and becomes my heartbeat.

Through our joint vessels
I pray for the stored wisdom
which has grown inside you
a multitude of years bygone...

My friend,
your image elicits a rain forest
of illusions and magic.
Soft green mossy beards and bodies
decorated with tree lace.
Now, giant tree wizards in eternal contemplation.

Your roots,
steadfast to our mother earth,
while heart and spirit inhabit the heavens.
A divine duality joined and balanced
by an elevated mind.

The tree lace Buddha looks down
and smiles upon the earth.

1980

A Soul Searching Journey

I continue to be amazed at the levels of reality that can be lived simultaneously. Programmed so thoroughly by years of societal training, the mechanics of living are often driven by a routine, which is embodied with an intrinsic knowledge and understanding of an ordered reality. In the midst of chaos and trauma, and even as diversion takes its course, the blueprints for an ordered reality remains. That is both a blessing and a curse, for the very order which is clearly the glue that allows for continued functioning can also be found to be the nemesis to healing and spiritual growth.

There is a time and place for everything, and living in tune with one's personal timing is the greatest blessing of all. My time of being carried through my crisis, by an ordered and tidy environment, was now up. It was time to stretch and take leave from my everyday life. Tim and I seldom traveled without one another or without the children. Part of the order that Tim and I created together involved the continuity of a strong, committed relationship and a cohesive family unit. That grew out of our genuine enjoyment of spending time with each other, and we were both so grateful to have found one another. Then, with children, our desire was to create a secure home environment that they could count on. My first challenge would be to allow myself to briefly step out of this norm, guilt free. That was actually easier than expected.

I always had a strong sense of self, and I was not one to lose my sense of personal identity even as my role might change. I recognized that all roles that one might take on in life are all part of the same whole self, and at that point in time my "self" was hurting. Since it was true that none of us are islands, my short absence from the nest would allow the rest of the family to also test their wings.

It all started as a simple comment by Jill, a dear friend and godmother to the children. It was April 1993. We had all made a trip to Oregon to visit family and friends. Jill flew in from Hawaii, where she lived for part of the year. Somewhere in our visit she suggested I join her in Hawaii for a week. Truthfully, Hawaii did not hold a lot of appeal to me at that time. Falsely, I just associated it with affluent tourists, of whom I was not one. Still, with just a little gentle coaxing it did not take long to realize how overdue I was for a bit of R and R. Hence, we completed our visit, returned home, and made arrangements for my next travel. With some trepidation about leaving Tim and the kids, I was scheduled to leave for Hawaii in May, just a few short weeks away. I knew it would encourage the acceleration of my personal resurrection, since I would have more time to focus on my bereavement needs. I looked forward to and anticipated the rebirth of more joy and light in my life. Jill agreed that we would not over schedule or over plan my stay. Perhaps a few short excursions to her favorite nature getaways, some shared time together catching up on some of the intimacies of our lives, and then much needed quiet and alone time for me. I had grown tired and saturated from the demands and stimulation of daily life. A reprieve from responsibilities sounded just right. After many hugs and several good-byes later I was off, feeling a strange combination of separation anxiety and the freedom to move at my own pace.

The flight to Hawaii was a long nine hours. With plenty of time for contemplation and relaxation, I sat in my own reveries and mused over the oddity of the crossing over time zones in travel and arriving so quickly at a different space. Being somewhat of a throwback to distant days and somewhat reluctant to join in on such a contemporary way of life, it was sometimes hard to grasp what a transient and mobile society we had become. As always I was intrigued with the concept of time and how fleeting and elusive it was. Unaccustomed to prolonged periods of inactivity in my life; I arrived in Hawaii rather crumpled and stiff. I marveled at those who could actually sleep for most of the duration of the flight, and at those who appeared much older than myself yet remained comfortable in their spot! As for myself, I was both tired and restless, and landing came none too soon. Seeing Jill, of course, brightened my spirits, while the hustle and bustle of airport activity brought my energy to attention.

The drive to Jill's held the enchantment that is always found when experiencing a new place for the first time. Being a person of fairly small stature and somewhat akin to my cold blooded friends, I was overjoyed to find the early morning air was already mildly warm and soothing to my skin. I was becoming suspicious that perhaps I had too quickly, and certainly too harshly, prejudged this tropical paradise as having nothing to offer for me. Upon seeing the water I was certain then of my poor judgment. Never before had I seen a body of water more turquoise blue or calming than this Pacific surrounding her islands. I could not take my eyes off of that beauty, which wasted no time before it permeated my soul and opened my heart to the expansion that would be necessary for my healing transformation. We spent the day with odds and ends of unpacking and settling in, which came before the leisure. Then the leisure emerged. I began to unwind as we shared snacks and chatted from up in her condominium where the view remained always immodest and present. The water was an ever present source of peace, as a place deep inside me responded to its vast and eternal qualities. Missing Tim and the children, and feeling disjointed from our separation, I was also reveling in the ability to slowly release the load that I had been carrying. There were times that I sat by the pool for hours and reverberated in deep repose. I didn't try to figure anything out but remained comfortably in the moment. There were stirrings dancing around inside and a clamor that would make its way to the surface, but I didn't try to rush it. I knew that it was not necessary to be in its pursuit, and that it would simply rise of its own accord.

In the meantime, I was comforted by the dreamy slow-motion state I was in, which felt just right for the moment.

On other occasions, Jill and I went to the ocean and walked along the beach, rescued an eel that had been washed ashore, looked for sea turtles, did Tai Chi in the early morning with water glittering beside us, went to lovely restaurants, and became childishly gleeful over the jungle-like banana trees and the great giant banyan trees. Already intoxicated by the water and slowness of life, my soul was being aroused and encouraged to break past the boundaries set by a rhythm that had once kept me afloat during great turmoil. It was time to rock the boat again.

Jill had plans for the evening. On my own I would let my spirit set the pace. I prepared myself for an evening of intensity. I called in the four directions, and asked for assistance with the next step on my healing journey. I prayed to be released from the pain that I no longer wished to hold and was eagerly ready to "give away" to the infinite power of love and compassion, to be transformed by that light and love. Through tears of grief and anticipation I called to Dad and told him that I loved him. More than anything I wanted to feel his presence, and then I would have to say good-bye to the old energetics of pain and suffering. I would tell him that I loved him, and that the time had come for him to move on and continue with his transition and new "life," and that I had to have my life back to be continued here on Earth, in a healthy manner. Those were hard words to say but I was strong and determined. Tim used to tell me that he was frightened that Dad would come to me and call me away. Not literally, of course, that would not happen. Dad was always my protector and he would never interfere. I think it was more the underlying energies of loss and longing that he was concerned would carry me off. Dad and I were like a sponge for each other's feelings, one that had not been rung out for a long time. I, however, loved my life and was committed to stay.

As those thoughts and feelings continued to unfold, the music in the background stirred my body to movement. I spread my wings and became Eagle, with shrieks of exclamation that announced my will to soar to new heights. My ribs and chest expanded and contracted with contortions and twisting movements. I was trying to literally step out of old patterns that had kept my body tired and sore. I prayed for help with the exertion of that pain and trauma, the effects of which needed to be eliminated from each and every cell in my body. I had done that hypnotically with suggestions for the removal of old imprinted messages, and now added to that message as I expressed it in dance and movement. My heart sang with a voice that was both melancholic and bold. My lips uttered words that I cannot remember. All was permitted to come forth and flow at will without question. My river had taken over and set the course for the evening's agenda. I needed only to allow that flow and trust in its process.

As the evening progressed I was eventually lulled into stillness and left to quietly resonate with the symbolic ritual surgery which I had performed. Though there would be more layers discovered at a future time, for the moment there had been a breakthrough and I was feeling the aftermath, resulting in being both tired and renewed. It felt good to be alone and silent. Surrendering to the heart and to the inner or higher self is an act of trust that can bring a new understanding of and an expanded relationship with *self*. It calls for another look in the mirror and a new attempt to really see who it is in the reflection. That new perception of the reflection will depend on the depth of the personal expansion that was experienced. At the very least there will probably be a reflection suggesting a strong sense of wonder about and respect for all the many dimensions which are felt but not seen, and perhaps a stronger commitment for seeking new wisdom and higher guidance. I continued the evening moving with an exaggerated grace and fluidity that befitted the new tenderness and intimacy with which I viewed my body. My body, with its own wisdom, which served as a sacred vehicle for moving me to a place of new understanding. The same body I had struggled with since birth and whose value I had denied had moved with spirit and had done well. Going to bed was welcomed and I slept with a deep ease that night.

The morning arrived with good cheer. There was breakfast and Tai Chi, and then down to the pool to sit in the sun and enjoy the warmth from the cosmos. Jill would arrive home soon and we would share the day together as quiet tourists. I would not review too thoroughly the events from the previous night but instead tuck them away for safe keeping. My time in Hawaii was coming to its end. In truth, it was a means to an end. I had faced the challenge of my dad's passing in a new and deeper way. Without distractions or excuses, I reckoned with my feelings and faced myself head on.

Was there something I could have done to save Dad? Can anyone really "save" another? I don't think so. Was it okay that I loved him enough that I could give him permission to go? Can I love myself enough to forgive whatever inadequacies I might have had or still have? Yes, yes to all of the above and much more. The business of healing is a lifelong process, as we grab at opportunities to strip away new layers that may present themselves. I knew that my job was not complete, yet I was more equipped to go home and keep with me the preciousness of my life and the life I had created with my family. It would be a joyful reunion.

Unity In Flight

A quiet spring day.
I strain to hear...
A cow moos passionately,
a child's voice, laughter,
a firecracker sounds like a rocket and whistles through space.
The wind chimes sing
 as a gentle breeze strokes the earth and cools the air.

Activity and stillness,
sounds and silence,
all at once fill my senses in unity, in harmony.
Nature's blend ignites my spirit,
and peace quickly gives way to lust and addiction.

I lust for the unity of geese in flight,
for the communion of the bees and the flower,
for the merging of the ballet dancers,
for the story told through the rings of a tree.

I want it all.
Never stopping creation flowing through my veins
and flooding my senses.
Awareness, communion with all energy, all life force.
A quiet spring day.
I lust for the unity of geese in flight.
It never stops...

1985

$\mathcal{U}$NITY

I returned home feeling lighter and freer than I had in years. Still somewhat dreamy and adjusting to time changes and all the little mind games that can happen when one moment we are in one part of the world and hours later we are again thousands of miles away. Taking the opportunity to travel away from home and care for myself was wonderful and rejuvenating to my spirit. Returning home to my warm and loving family and an assortment of our animal friends, including our floppy-eared Setter/Newfoundland mix whom we called Autumn, as well as the land already so lovely in the spring, was something to be very grateful for. It was all very satisfying and nourishing for me.

So I eased back into life in perfect timing with the re-birth of spring apparent everywhere, blushing in the shades of the wildflowers and annuals and swelling buds ready to burst. Tim and I were often busy in the garden, and that time with the earth again became my addiction. Meals were late, beading was put aside, and with the children either playing around me or napping, I was off to the garden. The garden, my sanctuary and healing room, was the drug necessary for quieting my lusting and thirsty soul. Even in my frenzy to single-handedly remove every weed that threatened to invade and mar the beauty, I heard all of the sounds around me. There were the ever present bird songs, the chirping of the insect world, and the rustling of the wind in the treetops. I smelled the smoke drifting from neighbors' distant burning leaves and the honey-sweet fragrance of the lilacs and honeysuckles. The breeze darted over my sweaty and muddied body, raising goosebumps even as the sun penetrated and warmed me once again. The children laughed and rattled with their wagonload of grass they had raked and then imagined to be hay for our goats. I planted and weeded and sucked in every ounce of the natural narcotic that buzzed my head and shook me loose from the earthbound human phenomenon of feeling separated from the rest of the natural world and from spirit realms. I often marveled at the polarities of my own existence. Though I undeniably loved the Earth with a passion, I was also a spirit that longed to fly. My passionate love affair with the earth actually served to fuel that flight. There would come a time in the future when, for continued and deeper transformation, I would have to put my longings to rest and more fully learn to enjoy living in my body. In the meantime, as my joy and love grew so did it fuel my need for higher realms and spiritual communion, and that would sometimes leave me feeling like a homing pigeon with a somewhat poor sense of direction still looking for home.

I always felt like I was in training for something more that I was to do here on Earth. Dream-time and awake-time alike, I was aroused and baited with more information. Insights, poetry, and truths were offered freely and automatically, and I didn't realize at the time how much they were relied on in my daily existence. It was never enough. I always wanted more. A channeler once told me that I had too much coming in at one time and that it was necessary for my well-being to ask for just one teacher to come forward and point out the pertinent information while filtering out the rest. I panicked at that thought when, in the next breath, I was told not to worry, that I would not miss out on anything important! I felt like I was being told to give up my right arm.

Sometimes I felt so close to breaking through the transparent barrier which separated me and restricted my communication with the whole broader scope of life. I could almost taste a new understanding permeating to the next level. My body and my soul remembered that esoteric ability, and my heart longed for it here on Earth. It seemed that when we came here to Earth we lost that direction. Focused largely on material survival, the course of higher understanding goes astray. My path and my drive targeted finding my way back to higher understanding and greater attunement, and to ground that here in my life on Earth. Clearly that had always been the design for my life. That path included building a life that made sense to me and was based on personal truths. That had been my motto for as long as I could remember. The world did not have many models reflecting a lifestyle for healthy living based on the integrity of being for mind, body, and spirit for facilitating harmony and balance. I would challenge myself and others to create and manifest that model, which could then be custom tailored and perfected throughout the course of a lifetime. That thought was like the gospel to me. It did not matter if I was teaching a class, seeing a private client, or enjoying friendly chatting amongst friends. It always came back to discussions about knowing ourselves well enough to know what was treasured and valued in life, and understanding where our passions lie and what tickled our fancy. That unveiling could then lead to discovering what made us tick, indeed, not the heart alone but the soul.

Soul work helps us to understand the intricacies involved in living which can lead to expanded awareness and satisfaction in life. Greasing the wheels for expanded awareness and transformation always circles us back to that soulful work. Intricate knowledge of *self* becomes the very grease that unlocks the gears that slide into action, and manifests into a living tide of motion presenting in the form of decisions and choices, and relationships and lifestyle, as well as communication and prayer. In many ways I had been doing soul work all of my life. Informal and sometimes unstructured, it led me down a path of love and creativity.

Reverie and philosophy felt distant when I plodded along with the wheelbarrow or dug in the flowerbeds. Instead, that summoned ancient calls and memories of survival on the land and contributing to the needs of a tribe. I thrilled in the instinctual pleasure of watching every little sprout's emergence and growth, and delighted in serving freshly gathered vegetables for dinner. The children were the bean pickers, and with baskets in hand they stretched high up for the beans at the top of the arched trellis. Each year marked how much they had grown by the highest bean they could reach, and as they would persevere in their reach for higher beans, I would exercise my ability to stretch into new horizons and beyond old limits. Familiar themes would reappear but with a deeper will for new understanding and expansion, and all of them traveled with me into the new year, especially my lifelong dream to help generate a foundation for "heaven on earth."

Silence Of The Dream Within

The sounds of the country
awaken the silence within.
A dream stirs.

A distant train rumble
shakes the earth.
Emotions are broken loose.

They follow the singing birds
and dart through the fields and sky.

The swirly clouds
paint peace and tranquility.
I am engulfed by the warmth
of the clouded sun.

A deep but patient sigh
serene, nagging, but quietly serene...
waiting.
The silence of the dream within.

1981

$\mathcal{T}$*HE* $\mathcal{E}$*TERNAL* $\mathcal{S}$*ACRED Dream*

I was sitting on the couch in the living room of a shaman who was delivering a talk on his experience with shamanism. Somewhere along the line he lost me. His words buzzed in the background. Preparations were being made for a journey to the upper world, a place where one can meet with their spirit guides. The drumming had not yet begun but I was already on the way. My body was beginning to change, to elongate. I was all in white. Words were still in the background but more and more distant. Out beyond the sliding glass door a large grizzly bear stood peering back at me. Next, I ascended to a precipice at Eagle's Rest (a beautiful overview hiking spot that Tim and I loved in Oregon) and stood there stating my intentions to travel to the upper world to meet with my teacher.

That was a common method used by shamanic practitioners. My stated intention was met by an explosion of energy as I burst through the membrane-like layer which separated the worlds and found myself cast into a frenzy of activity. Greeted by dancers in moose headdress, I sought out my teacher. Finally she appeared. Her brown hair, greased back and parted in the middle, was pulled tightly away from her long and narrow face. I couldn't really see her individual facial features, just the wholeness of her face. Still, I knew inside what she looked like. She had on flowing robes that went all the way to the ground. I asked for a healing and for an awakening to my true self and to *see* and learn all that I needed, which would permit me to benefit from the experience. I was thrust into a deluge of ceremony. My body was being pulled and stretched into what appeared as a long, flat ribbon. A buffalo came along with its head bent low. Many people were stamping the ground and sweeping the ground in a movement away from me. Sweeping away all traces of old footprints and old patterns? I wondered about these sensational movements, but was not disturbed. Into that exhilarating ceremony Eagle flew in, and I became captivated by the drumming, with the drum now being beaten by a bear's paw with enormous claws. Was this the bear that appeared to me earlier? Suddenly the drumming changed and I was whisked back down to Eagle's Rest and back to the room where I had started. My senses were flooded with remnants of the non-ordinary reality which I had glimpsed. I tried to capture the moment so I could reclaim it for future reviewing.

That experience served as an initiation for me into utilizing the art of shamanic practices as a resource for higher understanding and transformational healing. Up until that point I had been well versed at the academic level, and now I was ready to delve into the more experiential realm. I greatly enjoyed those times and found that they filled a spot within that had not been addressed in quite the same way.

As a child I had fears and greatly fretted over my feelings of vulnerability in regards to the spirit world. That was no longer true. Instead, I felt prepared and trusted in my powers and abilities as well as in the forces of light and love. I attended workshops, received private sessions, listened to drumming tapes, and honored my animal spirits and dreamtime teachers in every way that I could. Life became richer as I walked on Earth with even deeper feelings of compassion and tenderness and with the absolute certainty that I could emit and communicate that love. In a very real way all of the Earth became alive to me, and that which I once held to be true at the levels of faith and intellect became more of an experiential *knowing* as mind, body, and spirit became more unified. I sang to the fox that lived in a den under the barn and to my delight they came out to listen. I called to the birds that flew overhead, and held frequent negotiations with the woodchucks who ravished our garden. My medicine wheel, located in the garden, maintained its divinity throughout all seasons. Sometimes snow covered and at other times shrouded in flowers and herbs, it was held as a place for prayer, council, commitment, and affirmation ceremonies of intention. Gifted by the family with tobacco and corn, stones and flowers, it was used as a temple to voice joys and grieve losses, for dancing and singing to Grandmother Moon, and for shedding the invisible barriers which falsely separate humans from all of their relations.

Though not always understood by the children, I offered it as a model for spirituality, empowerment, and transformation. If we were to start our home-schooling day off on the wrong foot, we might go out to the medicine wheel and smudge away the old energies and thus be ready to begin anew. We all felt better as the wind would cleanse our anger or frustration and leave us uplifted and with the gift of renewed perspectives and options to explore. Most importantly, we would walk back to the house joyful and empowered to change the course of our day. If the children spied me alone at the medicine wheel they immediately recognized, perhaps not even consciously, that I was involved in prayer or some sort of sacredness, and they would either respectfully leave me to complete my activity or quietly come and stand by my side. There would always be time for them to speak their piece if so desired. In song or in silence they, too, could honor the mother for all of her treasures. I found it extremely important for them to learn to respect or at least tolerate the sacred space that someone might take for themselves, even if they themselves did not feel the same way.

There is a circle involving self respect and respect for others, or that which is internal and that which is external, which when maintained allows for a harmonious and satisfying existence on earth. One cannot learn to walk gently on the earth and with others until they have learned to be gentle with themselves and visa versa. I struggled with the idea of disciplining, until I came to the realization that a healthy approach to discipline includes being consistent in one's willingness to notice and to guide, along with a strong and present foundation of love, which when responded to by the children could translate into their personal power. Only when we have personal discipline, or the ability to use our will for our highest good, can we have the ability to embrace and create with self responsibility. My hope was that Shandra and Jacy would feel powerful and not overpowered in life, and confident in the possibilities available to them and created by them in their lives. I felt proud when they learned to recognize and respect my times of stillness, and hoped that their circle of respect, tolerance, and personal power gained through self discipline were being subconsciously understood and creating blueprints for a lifetime. Since we are not islands (thankfully), as mentioned earlier, the evolving spiral of one's spirituality can energetically produce a domino effect upon those with whom we are in a close relationship. Though it cannot be forced, an atmosphere that allows for individuality without the threat of denial, along with a consistent and persistent striving for the highest good for self and for others, becomes a gentle stroke in that direction.

Before having children of my own, becoming a parent was clearly a major part of my sacred and eternal dream. I went through a lot to get there, with four mysterious miscarriages and two years of infertility of unknown origin. Those were sorrowful times, when I longed for my motherhood. I had past-life memories involving losses of children, and felt certain that some pattern had to be broken. Finally, when I was pregnant again, I meditated and prayed, affirming my intention to surrender to the will of my higher self. I stated my intended promise to release all old karmic patterns and/or energy which limited me from successful conception and completeness, whether I knew what they were or not. I asked to be re-aligned with my higher self and re-attuned to that higher level of awareness and functioning. I carried those thoughts with me wherever I went. In the car, in the shower, cooking dinner, or at rest, they were never far away. Happily, I was graced with a normal and healthy pregnancy, including just enough morning sickness to assure me that my hormones were on track! I felt glorious in my full-term pregnancy and then birthed a beautiful 7-pound,

4-ounce little girl. I had my second child, my little boy, 21 months later. His conception was so easy that it was delightfully unexpected, as we just assumed we would not need birth control. So, when I started to have symptoms I thought it was just a bladder infection!

Motherhood and parenthood began without hesitation. With all the resolve and instincts that nature could instill, I began the trek that would prove to offer more opportunities to meet and face myself than I could ever have imagined. Angels and demons alike would emerge as I sought to maintain a true path--true to my commitment to help raise our children in the very best fashion of love that would nurture mind, body, and spirit, encouraging what was for their highest good while also weaving in some balance of what was for my highest good. At times that would be a juggling act that would change throughout the years, with new insights and abilities working their way to the surface and often presenting at unexpected times. There were times of uncertainty and even desperation as I worried over doing the "right" thing but always the pleasure of looking at my family and marveling at the realization that they were mine. There was seldom a day that went by where I did not stop and acknowledge the miracle of and deep gratitude for their creation. It was truly mind boggling and awesome to watch them develop, and to remember that we would continue to grow as a family for so many years to come. That idiosyncratic pondering over the miracles and intricacies of life was a passion that fruited me much pleasure, and also served to carry me over rugged terrain from time to time by keeping me more aware of the larger picture of life and ensuring a more balanced perspective.

I believe that we are all born with our unique, sacred dream essence living deep inside of us encased in a seed of light which retains all the memories and ancient knowledge from whence it was sown. That seeded dream, connected to our higher selves, offers the ability to live artfully, partially in higher realities and other dimensions as well as simultaneously in our normal, everyday dimension, and can filter in fragments of significant information with just the right timing. What an extraordinary paradox! While we as humans walk this Earth with very limited and narrow vision, pondering questions of creation or whether E. T.'s really exist or if time travel is possible, we continue to serve as the landladies and lords of souls who are involved in experiencing and living all of their lifetimes at once.

It follows, then, that the miracles so many are seeking are not to be found outside of themselves but within. Therein lies another directed piece of evidence that suggests the value of traveling the inner depths to find that gem of higher resource, with the intention of gaining assistance in releasing the old duality. In doing so we are freer to carry a wholeness of relationship with us in our lives on Earth. Though that may sound complicated, in truth it is found once again within the premise of honoring: honoring all of who we are and what we *know*, trusting in what we often call hunches and following through with what we know is true and right for us to do. Just like the image of mirrors reflecting one another for infinity, one step that we take will always illuminate the next.

We carry many seeds within us, all of which can become an expression. There are seeds of new life which can manifest as offspring of new hope. There are the seeds of fear and negativity which can become our demise. The sacred dream cradles the power of manifestations for seeds of light, which help in converting negativity to positivity. There are countless occasions available which, if so desired, can easily become opportunities for affirming and celebrating the positive aspects and attributes of life. Each morning's sunrise reflects an offering for a new beginning. The monthly full moon elicits the desire to exuberantly move past the earlier limits of old thinking and perspectives. New years and new seasons, birth and rebirth, coming of age and birthdays all cry out to be honored, and merit the time spent in revisiting and re-crystallization of the dream. When living mindfully and awake, each meal shared becomes a reminder of life cycles and the beauty of the *give-away*, with one life (be it vegetable or animal) sustaining another. We need not build upon an illusory division when preferably we can nourish a dream of wholeness and completeness.

It is true that life on Earth often places shadows on the dream that can keep it hidden in dark and seemingly forbidden places. That truth is simply part of the challenges and lessons that Earth provides, and it does not discourage the dream as it does the dreamer. The dream waits and remains safe within its light haven. There are no time frames for when it must be birthed. However, I as the dreamer have grown impatient and frustrated on numerous occasions. After all, what point is there in playing a game where all the rules are not understood? It can feel like we are playing out a personalized micro-version of the light versus dark theme of the universe. It takes a lot of work to keep one's spirits up and plug along in the race where the outcome remains open to an uncertain victor. It comes down to trust once again, and to the realization that investment in the outcome of an action is just a distraction, and that's the real beauty. There are no promises or rewards immediately visible or extrinsically valuable when walking a path with heart. The value is truly intrinsic and will not buy fame, fortune, or even outside acknowledgement. For me, there is no choice. I must and will always make an effort to walk a path with heart even on days of feeling disheartened. My dream is eternal. It has a mind and a fire of its own, and connected to the infinite flame, it will not die.

I am thinking of late summer of 1993. The days were still warm, but the evenings hinted of the coming fall. The summer had been renewing and I felt prepared to face the challenges of the pending autumn. The structure involved in being a home-schooling family for us paralleled the motion of the seasons. The outer flow in life becomes curtailed as reigns are pulled in and buckled down, and energy is harnessed to last through the winter. First, though, there would be a trip to Crystal Lake, one of our favorite little getaways near Sleeping Bear Dunes in Michigan. True to its name, the lake is sparkling and still, and inspires both reflection and excitement. It is small enough so the children can easily behold its breadth and shorelines yet large enough to offer a stimulating view. This time we would share a cabin with friends, which satisfied my desire for extended family and the feeling of communal kinship.

There were eight of us--four adults and four children--an even match. What could have been hectic determined to run smoothly. It felt good to be four cooperating adults sharing and preparing pleasant meals and conversation; along with four children enjoying being children. We hiked in the birch tree groves and looked for an old chestnut orchard. Birch paper decorated our path and tree frogs skipped along from row to row. The children echoed charming words of delight. I took note of their pleasures and their choice of words, and later turned them into poetry. I wanted them to experience the power and magic of their heart-spoken and written expressions. When we returned home I surprised them with a poem written for each of them using their own phrases for their deepened memories of the trip. The kids and I would write many poems together in the coming year, many of them mirroring our observations of the natural world.

As our trip came to an end, we said our good-byes to our even closer friends and parted company, each family returning in their own directions. Back as a family unit we traveled in our capsule (car) and arrived home at the farm in what seemed like no time. I remembered again the need for tribal and village life. Perhaps at some point in the future, for humanity's survival, it will have to come to that community life again. For the moment, however, I was renewed from the spirit of kinship and cooperation between friends and ready to continue with the challenges we face in a smaller, nuclear family framework.

In many ways I have always been a self-contained person in that I enjoy my personal time and am seldom at a loss as for what to do. There is so much that brings me pleasure in life. Still, regardless of how well I adapted to the modern world and western style of living, there remained the faint knowledge that something was off base or askew. I was usually the happiest when I ignored that message and committed to creating the most that I could within the limits of a structure that was somewhat inadequate. Being present with my joy and also in pursuit of expanded new vision, I could see beyond the inadequacies and learned to continue aspiring to the larger picture, which held a larger understanding.

There are moments, even days, when I can sense the larger picture and keep it with me comfortably tucked in a spirit pocket where I can reach far into its depths and truly feel it as tangible. Those are moments of pure pleasure and they usually shine a new light on an old vision of my reality. Really, that new insight is often all it takes for facilitating a thoughtful shift in the perceptions of our reality or circumstances. It does not take an earthquake to make that shift, which then becomes a gateway for love, compassion, trust, and contentment. To some the sound of contentment conjures up images of inertia and apathy—like the round old mouse from the story of Jumping Mouse by Hyemeyohsts Storm who grew increasingly fat and satisfied each day with an abundance of berries and herbs available to him and thus did not choose to seek or journey to the sacred mountains, as did the true hero of the story, Jumping Mouse himself. I do not equate that manner of lethargic behavior with the contentment to which I refer, but rather as a reflection of the loss of spirit that is so prevalent in the world. The contentment I refer to permeates all levels of self and is rooted in a higher understanding and awareness, which then translate into a more peaceful experience of life on earth. As negativity and urgency are released, trust, patience, and hopefulness are re-established and energy is regained. Energy that once was drained by negativity and overload can be freed and used for healing purposes. Some people fear that the jargon that goes along with discussions about spirituality, such as energy, wholeness, light, love, grace, and so on, serve only to blind people to the ills of the world. My experience has been contrary to such thinking. In a spiritual relationship, made stronger in unity, we can find a clarity and a determination to participate as active and empowered co-creators, facilitating the transformation necessary for healing the Earth and all of her inhabitants.

I Am The Quiet Of The Falling Snow

Twin Sisters

What does it matter if "this" is an illusion or reality?
You and I together, here and now,
creating reality or illusion for each other.

For our journeys, our peace of mind, our pleasures, and
for our lessons, even our pain.

Illusion and reality, the twin sisters equally strong,
both capable of inducing joy and well-being,
and harsh enough to bring us to our knees,
crying and demanding for the sisters to express
the warmth and compassion of which they are capable
at all times!

The dreams, the dreamer, reality, and illusion
all just words for the same miraculous and tumultuous expression
and experience of that which is and shall ever be.

2001

I Am The Quiet Of The Falling Snow

$\mathcal{T}$ WIN SISTERS

The twins of life are the dualities which remain a constant theme that serves to keep us from the wholeness of life of which we are a worthy part. Illusion or reality, dreamtime or wake time, earth or spirit are all linguistic representations of an existence that is black or white, and illustrates a thought process which denies the continuum in which we live. I have always sought to perpetuate wellness and healing transformation, heaven on earth, and purity of existence within perimeters which, by their own definition and nature, are finite, narrow, and blinding. So one might wonder, How do we facilitate a broader existence when what is required for its success must be expansiveness, even while our life on earth is entrenched in materiality that can easily negate that?

Healing or unifying mind, body, and spirit can begin with the feeling that it is an arduous and challenging journey filled with doubts and questions, such as, Will I make it? Will I succeed? Will I know what to do? Questions of doubt can try to invade the psyche, promoting self-perpetuating fears and disharmony. The narrow perspective and force that binds us to a reality of separateness does not give way easily. It will remain dominant if not taught, directed, and commanded by love's superior authority to break down barriers, release us of fear, and promote the opportunities for seeing, knowing, and trusting to occur.

I remember sitting by a flowing water fountain in a little quaint coffeehouse, in a small and not so quaint town. I was drinking a cup of very hot tea cooled down with ice. I wandered around looking at cards and journals which invited and stimulated memories. I moved so slowly and relaxed, enjoying the easy pace and freeness of the moment. I allowed the peace and stillness to permeate me like a gentle caress, reassuring my soul that I was paying attention to the current altered state of perception. I noticed the subtle nuances that brought pleasure to my spirit, and let my mind/body awareness memorize and learn to hold that quiet place. In those times of stillness and harmony there is an opening, a window available, through which one has the opportunity to experience the "Twin Sisters" as one. When that occurs, awareness has heightened and broadened enough to allow for a deepened familiarity with non-linear and expanded thinking, thus enhancing the exploration of concepts which can lead to more multidimensional experiences of life. As the veil of separateness or dualities softens, it evokes much joy and harmony. That, in turn, serves to awaken higher knowledge and wisdom, and an abundance of energetic creativity which can be offered as a gift both to one's self and humanity.

With so much happening in the world, it is commonly asked, "What can one person do to help?" It is easy to understand why so many people who feel powerless and overwhelmed live in more of a "sleep state" than a real alive and awake state. Sometimes that can be easier, and for many it may be the only way to function and keep up with the daily tasks of survival. That is truly understandable and even necessary, especially for those who have not acquired the skills or tools that can help them release pain while maintaining clarity and the ambitious belief of hopefulness that life really can get better. However, though it may seem beneficial to sleep through life's less than pleasant moments, the unfortunate side effects from that remedy include being excluded from the satisfaction which comes from successfully entreating new awareness about the power of love and unity. The realization and acknowledgement about the powerful force of a unified mind, body, and spirit can be appreciated more, as one continues on a personal growth journey to their sacred and higher self.

One sincere person has so much to offer. Each of us has the capacity for love, compassion, empathy, and generosity of spirit. Those are concepts which come from thoughts, and thoughts are energetic waves that create an effect, and waves can travel. Waves of energy are not restricted by the indefinite boundaries of time and space designed by humans desperate to define their reality. Waves of love and thoughts of peace and the possibility of creating a better world are limitless and without restriction. With intentional direction they can arrive at a destination, perhaps at the bedside of an ailing friend or beside a mother and child in some war-consumed country, depleted of all hope and tired of existence. You may counter and say that one person cannot support the world, and that not everyone has those tremendous "supernatural" abilities. I am delighted to address that point; in fact, it is hard to suppress my enthusiasm. It makes me want to raise my voice loud and clear and to wail with exuberance because it is so important to remember.

We are not islands, as I have said before. We are connected, and there is nothing that we have to do to make it so--it simply is! We are connected to each other, to waves of energy, and to great healing forces, and that in itself gives us the power to help. Each of us can sit at home alone and pray or meditate, and send the intention for love and peace to spread across the Earth. Then, very importantly, we can learn to live with love and generosity, and to live in the world, as we want it to be. Magnify that effect by knowing that hundreds, even thousands of people around the world are doing the same thing. You may not be able to see them all and you may not know who they are, but they are there. They exist and they are trying to make a better world too, just like you. Remembering that we are one, part of the same world and the same infinite energy field, participating with the same intentions for love and peace: just remembering that will magnify the power of your intention and the amount of joy that you receive. When you are ready you can leave your home and sit in circles with others doing the same thing, and feel the boundaries of self/aloneness dissolve as your energies of intention combine and become one. Some call this the power of prayer, yet the power is not only outside of the self but deep inside within our sacred hearts. As we find our power and merge with others, we are then establishing the ever powerful critical mass needed to truly change the world. Does one need supernatural abilities for connecting with that personal love power and with others? No; with self-exploration and willingness, each will discover a new superabundance of natural abilities that are indeed very simple. They've always been there, just waiting to be recognized.

Love Is The Miracle

It is not magical or supernatural
or voodoo or such.
There is no mystery, it is plain for all to see,
to know, to feel and taste and touch, and such.

It is not limited to rich or poor,
there are no boundaries
and there can be no petty theft or power struggle.

Love is the miracle.
It is not written on a billboard
though I do not know why.

Love is the miracle.
It will not be seen online or in magazine advertisements
or TV commercials
though I do not know why.

It is not taught in schools or discussed by talk show hosts.
Doctors do not prescribe it

and pharmacies do not stock it
though I do not know why.

Love is the miracle. Repeat these words.
Love is the miracle, it is not an unknown factor.

So, factor love into life.
Breathe love, drink love, eat love,
give away love, receive love,
re-use, remit, but never never remove love.

Be love because love is the miracle.
Be love when you are buying groceries,
riding your bicycle,
working in the garden, meeting with business clients,
seeing patients or better still, seeing people,
cleaning your dog's yard and sweeping the floor.

Breathe it in. Love is the miracle.
Let tiny messengers of sparkling chi bubbles
permeate every cell of your body,
carrying the light, carrying the word, the new word,
the new message.
Love is the miracle that all can receive.

2004

I Am The Quiet Of The Falling Snow

$\mathcal{L}$ove Is the Miracle

It was one of those nice relaxed days when I was walking back from the garden, and I was paying attention to moving slow and releasing all urgency. I was remembering to be part of the great infinite chi field, with my head touching the beautiful blue sky and my feet going all the way through the earth to the blue sky on the other side (an image taught to me by my Chilel Qigong instructors, Luke and Frank Chan). My mind was quiet and dreamily meditative, and I was filled with a gentle joy of life. As I often did at those times, I made a silent prayer that the day would come when everyone on Earth would have the opportunity to experience the profound pleasure in life that comes from having a sense of well-being, peace of mind, and beauty in life. While I hesitate to name such feelings as luxuries, because they are so essential to a positive existence, I cannot help but recognize that for many people around the world who are struggling to survive, those moments of gratitude may seem illusive or questionable at best.

With all of those thoughts and awareness, hopes, dreams, and prayers floating around unobtrusively in my mind, I continued walking gently on my way. Those thoughts did not steal my peace as much as they nudged me forward to surrender to a higher reality that was filled with resolutions and solutions. What was it that I heard? *"Use your love, love becomes chi."* Yes, that was it, use your love and love becomes chi. Chi, the invisible life force that flows through all living beings and becomes one in the infinite field of love and compassion. Chi which, like energy waves, flows with intention, direction, intelligence, and without judgment. Like the river flowing from one source to join unwaveringly with her ocean, chi flows through all life while maintaining connection to the infinite source of all life.

I understood that chi was the manifestation of love's living power to transform. Chi being the energetics that supports love in its desire to perpetuate harmony and balance in the universe, I began to think of chi as the creative heart of the universe, perhaps even the heart of the God/Goddess energy itself. That became so clear to me as I also began to realize that, while we are all searching for that miraculous fountain of youth or for a miraculous healing, it was always there deep within our sacred hearts, just waiting for us to learn to access it. I thought about clients I had worked with combining hypnosis and chi energy work, which I called Hypnochi. More importantly, I remembered the way I felt inside, especially during those times when they were experiencing extreme benefit. Those were times when I was "told" what to do, and where my "connection" or access to love was so profound that my joy was almost painful or overwhelming. Sometimes those clients would call me on the phone to say that their symptoms were gone, even a life-threatening tumor! I would hang up the phone and call for my family so I could share and explain about the power of love, and then I would cry throughout the course of the day. I cried with awe and deep respect for the loving and compassionate force of the infinite chi field that had touched me and allowed me to be a vehicle for its wondrous work.

I knew then that love was the miracle, and understood that once humans could learn how to hold that love and access it at will, miracles which once seemed so out of reach would then be available. Of course, that would be the bringing of heaven to Earth, which had been my dream in life--the joining of heart, mind, body, spirit, and infinity in a complete unity, all for what I call Intentional Well-Being. Harmony, love, and balance already exist. It is not necessary to dig a new well to find them. Within chaos there is a harmonic overflow that is the undercurrent, which is always ready to move into action to steady one's course. It is not felt through panic but is put into action through love that becomes the energy of chi, which is the creative power of the infinite flow, and in that way becomes a sacred dance of life. Circles and spirals, vortexes and six-pointed stars, infinity wheels and yin/yang designs are all depictions of harmonized movement and flow, illustrations of the connectedness and unity in life.

All of the above brings us right back to the beginning, that is, the question, What can one person do? I do not have all the answers, but I do have some thoughts. For instance, for starters we can commit to our lives. We can believe that there is something better, something more to life than what meets the eye, and we can choose to pursue a life with that ideal in mind. That means we would agree to do our best and to be our best, to search for and acknowledge our special gifts and then use them for ourselves and for the betterment of humanity. Some might tell you that it is indulgent and selfish to spend time looking for personal "gifts" and finding satisfaction, or that self-care is too self-centered. I would tell you differently, bearing in mind first that life is a balance, and even the pursuit of higher understanding and satisfaction must be done within the framework of that which is good for the individual and the whole, which is the goal. Next, I would suggest that it is a significant undertaking and even a necessity for each of us to remember that we are sacred and have a purpose for currently being here on Earth. The talked-about critical mass needed for saving humanity, the Earth, and all beings accumulates person by person and comes through self-exploration and the willingness to grow. Without introspective contemplation, thoughtfulness, and personal attention, how would one begin to recognize what felt authentic to them and thus brought them joy? Joy is ecstatic, dynamic, alive, and contagious. One can feel it, see it, and just about taste it as it grows and breathes within. It is a tangible entity which is both the embodiment of and an expression of love. Joy is the knowing of peace, well-being, and trust, and though it may be fleeting it leaves a residue of hope and promise. Have you ever met a truly joyful person who was not also generous? Or noticed someone who really loved what they were doing? It's so obvious because that person stands right out, and it feels good to be around them. Someone who has found satisfaction and contentment in what they are doing is usually helpful, cooperative, courteous, and reasonable. Though that list could go on and on, please notice the absence of *selfish*. It takes time to figure out who we are and what makes us tick, and what is pleasing to our spirit. It also takes effort and a clear commitment to do so.

We could for a moment look at what results when the reverse is true and one simply drifts along blindly, that is, blind to one's true self and empty of connection. Just look around, read the newspaper, or listen to the news. Statistics about abuse, drug use, debt, violence, depression, suicide, lack of respect for the environment, corruption, and the true fear-based selfishness of greed all serve to illuminate the results of a joyless and self-less life. It is important to understand that our true self is a connection to spirit or alignment with spirit, and that is the connection which inspires harmony and balance on Earth, which is what healing transformation is about both for the individual and for the Earth.

I can remember being at an intensive workshop on Shamanism where we were talking about illness manifested in mind or body, and how it might be perceived by ascended teachers and masters. We were asked to *journey* about that matter, which required leaving behind the old boundaries of limited thinking and expanding into both the inner and outer dimensions to meet with our teachers for the purpose of receiving insights on that question. With drumming and chanting to assist with that transition I soon found myself with my teachers and prepared to voice my question, and so I asked, "What is it that you perceive to be occurring in the body when I ask you about illness?" Here is what I received in response:

"There is an ebb and flow in a large infinite picture that is all inclusive and flawless in the larger picture of existence. An example of this could be a large piece of leather or fabric that was perfect in its infinite wholeness though changes in its grain could be perceived. When one speaks of perfection in wholeness, it is comprised entirely of symbiotic relations or flow. When one perceives of and speaks of illness, I perceive a lack of

symbiotic flow or harmony which then reflects fear and the perception of
separation. So when one speaks of illness I perceive disharmony and fear
relationships (cellular) which no longer work symbiotically."

So, it sounded as though illness was a reflection of the disconnect between mind, body, and spirit that is often associated with the human experience, where the body's wisdom, the mind's thoughtful intentions, and the spirit's insights have not been able to unite and manifest a symbiotic relationship that would be for the highest good. It is good to remember that there is no fault to be named or blame to be taken. It has simply been the stage for our human experience and the instrument for our continued human development. We are not a stagnant population without possibilities and potentials. The beauty lies in remembering that being connected to the great macrocosm gives us of the microcosm infinite room to grow and learn and to enhance life. So what seems infinitely confusing and seemingly out of reach, becomes simplified and reachable one step at a time down the road of *becoming*. It is also very comforting to note that since there is no finish line it must also be true that there is no race. What that means is that there is no hurry and there is no comparison to others. Our journey's growth and development is only relative personally to where we began. Take great joy in knowing that all any of us have to do in life is what we can in each moment, and no more. That knowledge encourages the simple commitment to allow ourselves to be and do our best every step along the way, keeping in mind that new possibilities for healing transformation are available every step along the way. In essence, every step and every day can be a fresh new start. We are free to choose a road; see where it leads, and discover what it has to offer. The transformation lies in how we respond to the unknown riddles of life.

This Dirt Road

Ah, this dirt road breathes deep sighs of peace and joy,
quietude and solitude,
and whispers the footsteps of
deer and rabbits and so many brothers and sisters
that scurry about with the pleasure of sweet earth
between their hooves and toes.

This dirt road is graced by the shadows of
sandhill cranes gliding, clacking, laughing overhead
red-tailed hawks screeching their presence, and
red-winged blackbirds flitting from tree to tree.

And the creek meanders over, under, across
and sometimes swims the width of road
while cattails stand their ground in swamps and
frogs have won anew arenas,
and this dirt road offers a soft gentle bed for

those little beings awaiting a new day
to emerge once again.

This dirt road emerges again relieved by its
spongy, springy, tender body
that no longer sends dust to sting the eyes
and fill the nostrils of all animals who alight upon this road,
but instead now receives the feet with a velvet touch
to cushion and help them along their way.

Listen, this dirt road tells the story of
dogs astray and woodchucks announcing
that spring has arrived this very day,
of horses and humans sharing relationship and companionship
as little children smile upon their backs and
wave to neighbors who lift their heads out of flower beds
to say good day good day.

And sometimes it holds the memory of the cat
with lovely stripes or colors of black and white
who did not make it home that night,
while the flashlights searching and yearning
illuminated the tears that streaked the faces and the glimmer of hope

that was left with the footsteps now etched
in the memory of this dirt road.

Let us not forget the secrets that sworn never to reveal
this dirt road buries deep within its layers
perhaps about the children at last free
to hurry recklessly on wheels making grooves
within this dirt road, or the friends that wander carefreely
and mingle stories and share their truths,
or the lovers holding hands and speaking dreams
and fears and words not said before
that come out freely and safely between them and
leave behind a trace of romance that fairies catch
and then shriek in playful ecstasy.

2003

And so the quiet road unravels many truths and many wonders to each to find in their own way and at just the right time. With just a little willingness mixed with a bit of readiness, pieces of understanding are extended and with free will enter the place in the great vast puzzle that was meant just for them. As it is with time and space continuums, there are no beginnings and there are no endings, and so those truths are given and discovered in a non-linear fashion, which make for a patchwork quilt of higher understanding that stunningly affects the whole fabric regardless of its placement. That is quite ingenious since it allows for all happenings to be meaningful and for something in all experiences to be of value. We are free to forget about regrets and not to agitate over "mistakes" but rather to enjoy peace of mind in trusting that they too will find their proper place in the great scheme of things, even if unbeknownst to us at the time. As we step into that great body of trust and peace, so do we also receive the blissful quiet found only in one's satisfied soul.

I Am The Quiet Of The Falling Snow

I am the quiet of the falling snow
shifting through the layers of dimension without distortion
while fragments of old reality shatter and suspend judgment
as all possibilities kaleidoscope about in abundance
and in anticipation of all potentiality.

I am the quiet of the falling snow
in the breathlessness of astonished wonder
as chills of beauty so profound
announce the hairs on my arm
now standing straight up
in speechlessness quietly exquisite
as my footsteps are met by the surrendering earth
allowing and permissive of my touch.

I am the quiet of the falling snow
crystallizing in shiny dewdrops on webs

of interlacing networks crisscrossing through the eons
on the backs of design messenger patterns
elaborately displayed in the horizon
yet subtle to the naked and unknowing eye.

I am the quiet of the falling snow
serenely dipping through the holes in time
and melting into chambers
with glistening receptors
enchanted with the notion of deciphering
if only for that instant
the mysteries that are found in the template of illusion.
I am that quiet of the falling snow.

1999

www.ingramcontent.com/pod-product-compliance
Lightning Source LLC
Chambersburg PA
CBHW052003090426
42741CB00008B/1523